perpetual

rita wong
cindy mochizuki

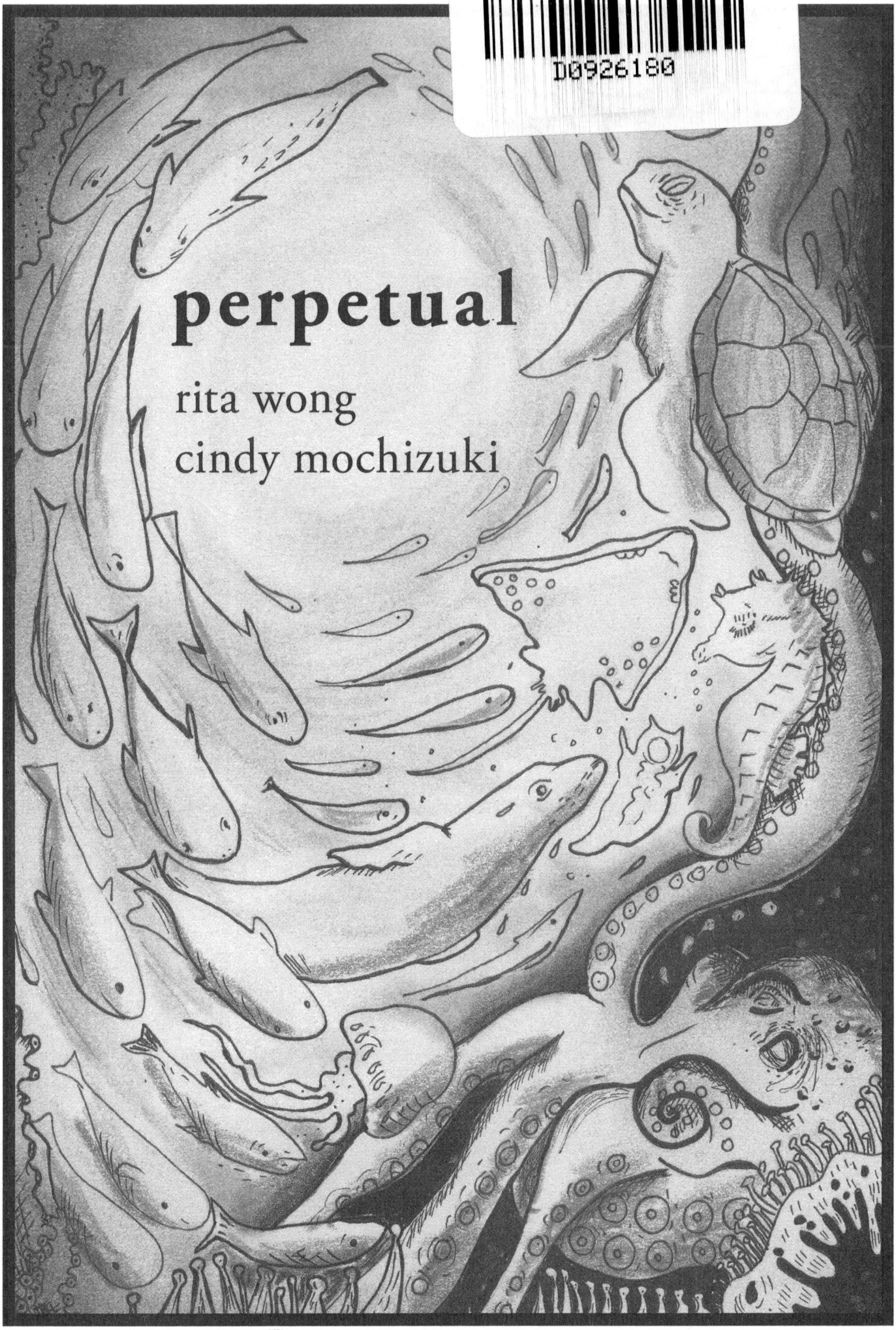

NIGHTWOOD EDITIONS
2015

Nightwood Editions
P.O. Box 1779
Gibsons, BC V0N 1V0
Canada
www.nightwoodeditions.com

COVER & INTERIOR ILLUSTRATIONS: Cindy Mochizuki

Canada Council   Conseil des Arts
for the Arts   du Canada

BRITISH COLUMBIA
ARTS COUNCIL
An agency of the Province of British Columbia

Nightwood Editions acknowledges financial support from the Government of
Canada through the Canada Book Fund and the Canada Council for the Arts,
and from the Province of British Columbia through the British Columbia Arts
Council and the Book Publisher's Tax Credit.

This book has been produced on 100% post-consumer recycled, ancient-forest-
free paper, processed chlorine-free and printed with vegetable-based dyes.

Printed and bound in Canada.

CIP data available from Library and Archives Canada.

ISBN 978-0-88971-313-0

dedicated to the health of your
spirited waters, dear readers

for all readers, big and small

water as poetics & praxis

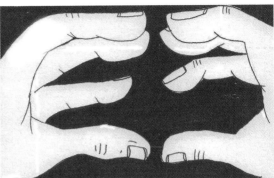

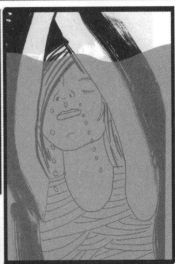

① Imagine the spaces in ①
② which you live through the ①
① lens of water. You are part ①
② of the hydrological cycle, this ②
planet's crucial circulatory
system. Your brain is roughly
85% water, your body approximately
70%, depending on your
age (more if you are younger, less
if you are older.)

From one perspective, Vancouver is an urban centre;

modernized, industrialized and gentrified by global capital and labour.

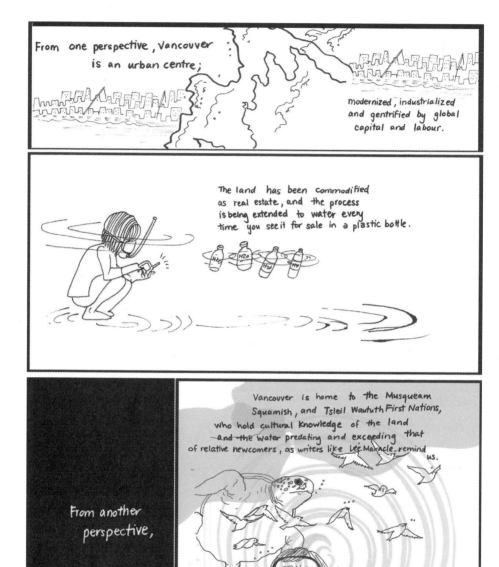

The land has been commodified as real estate, and the process is being extended to water every time you see it for sale in a plastic bottle.

From another perspective,

Vancouver is home to the Musqueam Squamish, and Tsleil Waututh First Nations, who hold cultural knowledge of the land and the water predating and exceeding that of relative newcomers, as writers like Lee Maracle remind us.

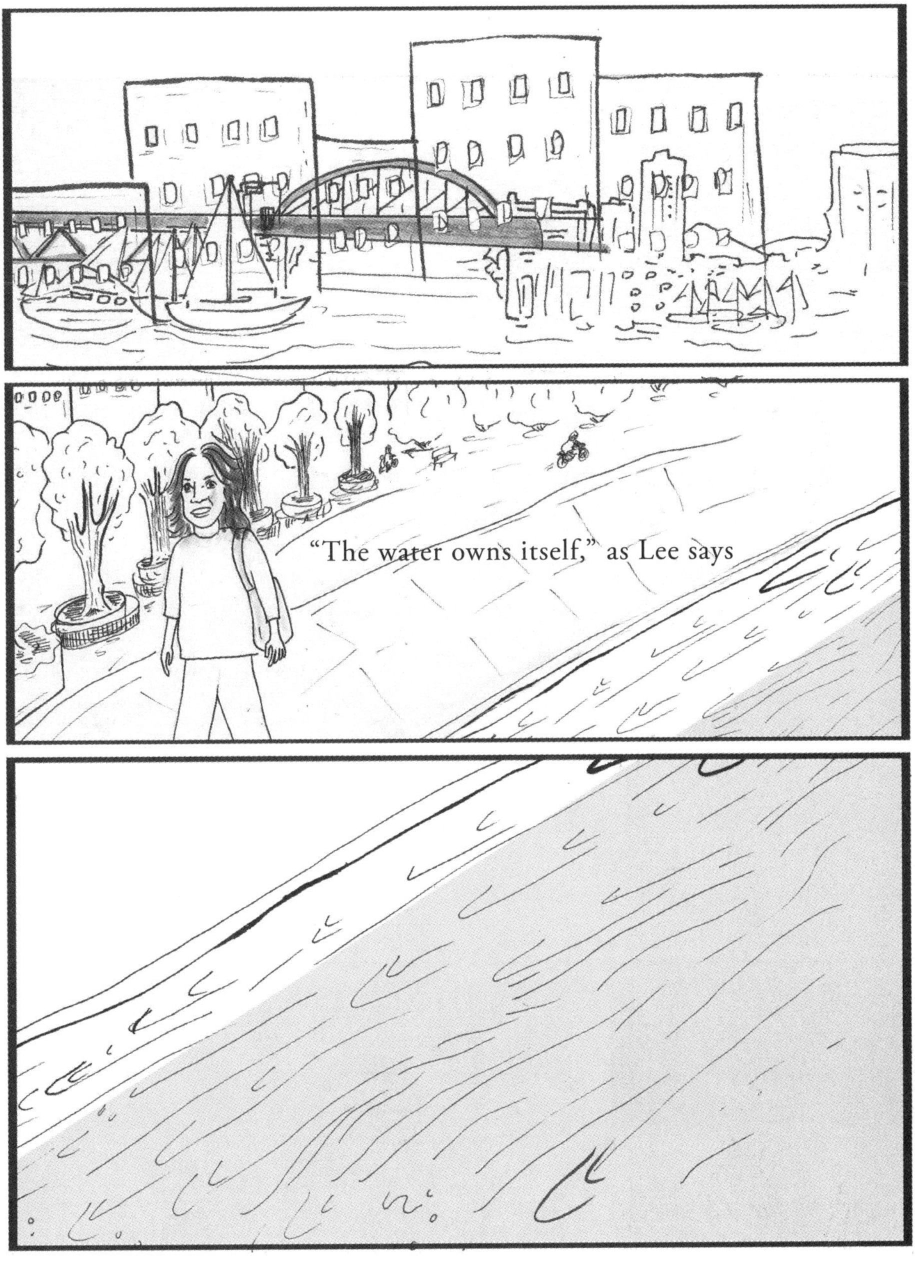
"The water owns itself," as Lee says

st stream walks lost stream wa

In September, I went on a number of lost stream walks organized by Celia Brauer and the False Creek Watershed Society, and now when...

I walk Vancouver's streets, I cannot help but listen for dips and cracks in the ground that might signal stubborn streams underneath.

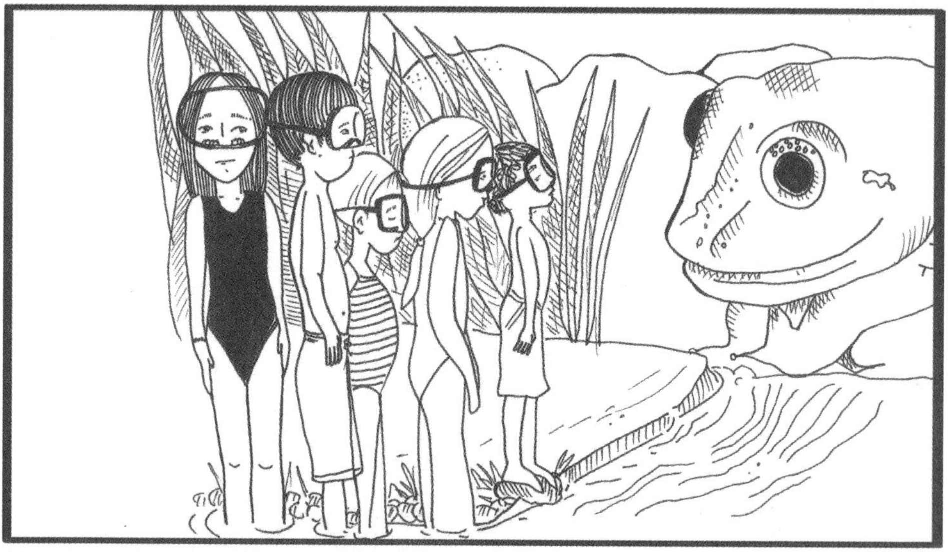

I live near a small stream that was paved over.

I can hear it,

under the manhole covers around 5th & St. George, stubbornly flowing.

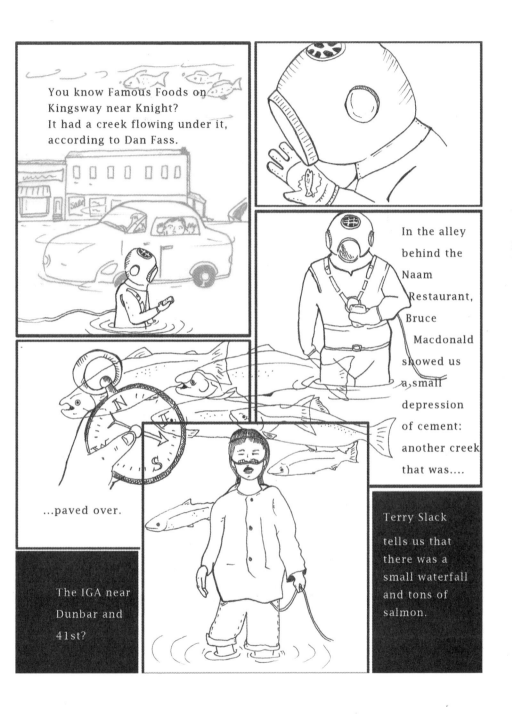

You know Famous Foods on Kingsway near Knight? It had a creek flowing under it, according to Dan Fass.

In the alley behind the Naam Restaurant, Bruce Macdonald showed us a small depression of cement: another creek that was....

...paved over.

The IGA near Dunbar and 41st?

Terry Slack tells us that there was a small waterfall and tons of salmon.

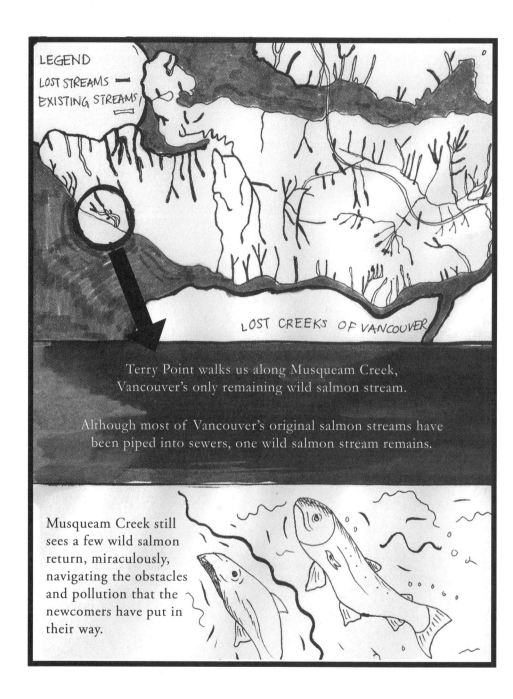

LEGEND
LOST STREAMS —
EXISTING STREAMS

LOST CREEKS OF VANCOUVER

Terry Point walks us along Musqueam Creek, Vancouver's only remaining wild salmon stream.

Although most of Vancouver's original salmon streams have been piped into sewers, one wild salmon stream remains.

Musqueam Creek still sees a few wild salmon return, miraculously, navigating the obstacles and pollution that the newcomers have put in their way.

Creek lovers in Saltwater City (what the Chinese called Vancouver) also hear the call of the water.

Each day when I bike past
the buried stream

I hear it gurgling its
longing to return to
daylight & moonlight

to nurture ducks
& bracken ferns &
salmonberry & people.

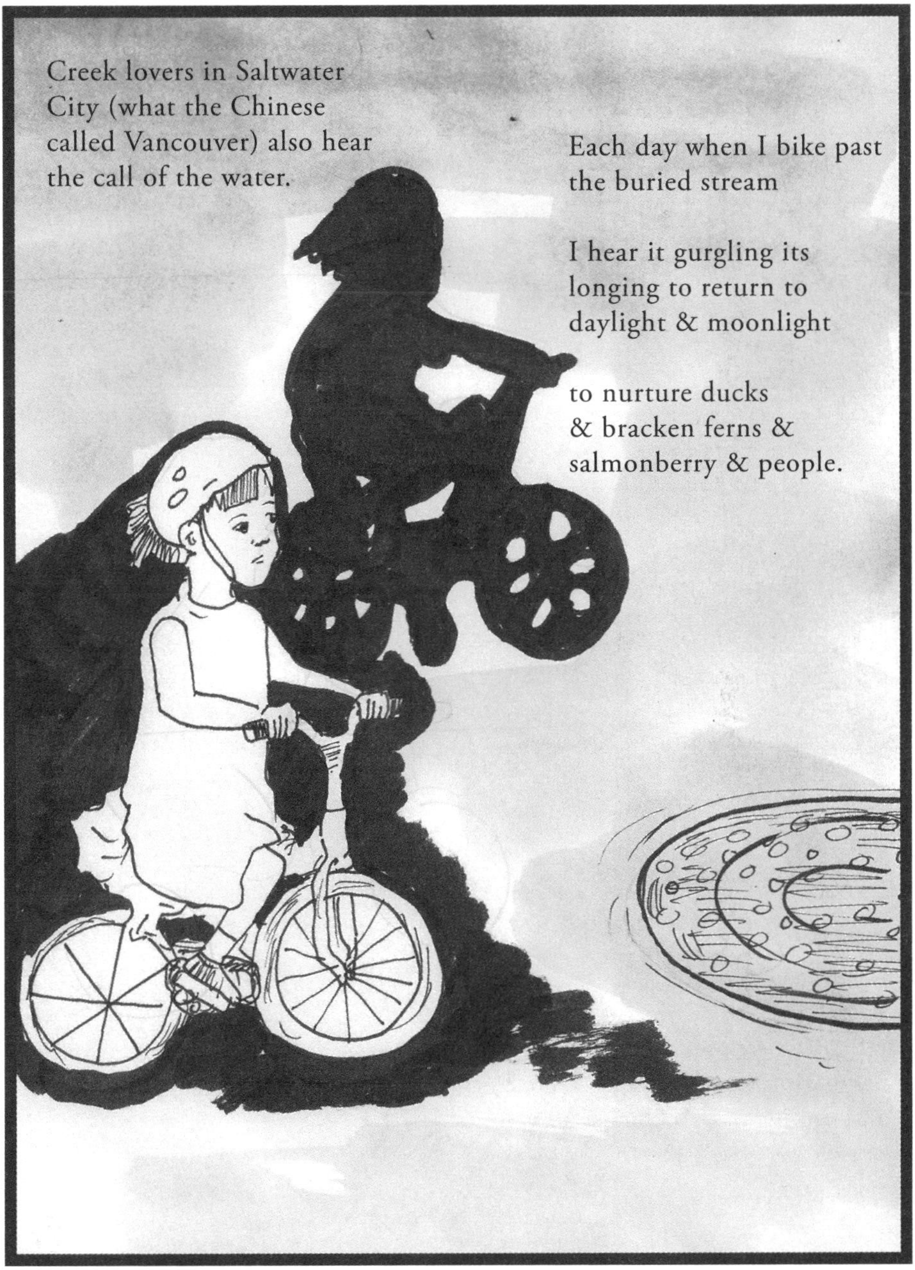

In the neighbourhood of Mount Pleasant, people try to reconnect to the buried creeks.

Tə Statləw, also known as the St. George Rainway, has brought them together.

Great Northern Way Campus

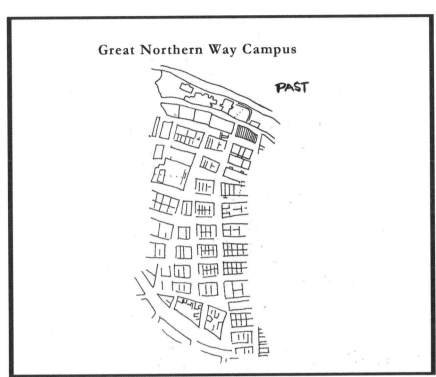

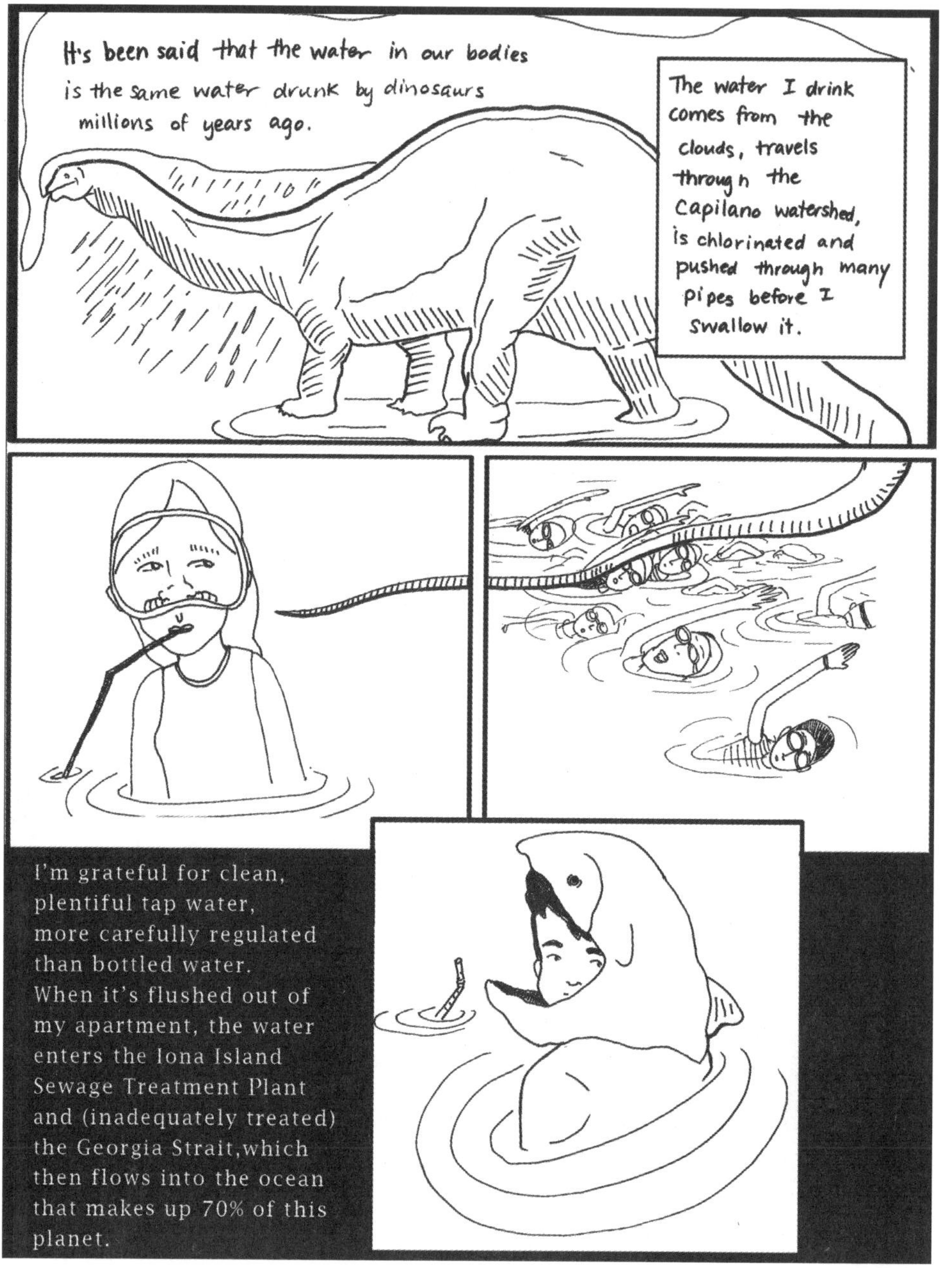
It's been said that the water in our bodies is the same water drunk by dinosaurs millions of years ago.
The water I drink comes from the clouds, travels through the Capilano watershed, is chlorinated and pushed through many pipes before I swallow it.
I'm grateful for clean, plentiful tap water, more carefully regulated than bottled water. When it's flushed out of my apartment, the water enters the Iona Island Sewage Treatment Plant and (inadequately treated) the Georgia Strait, which then flows into the ocean that makes up 70% of this planet.

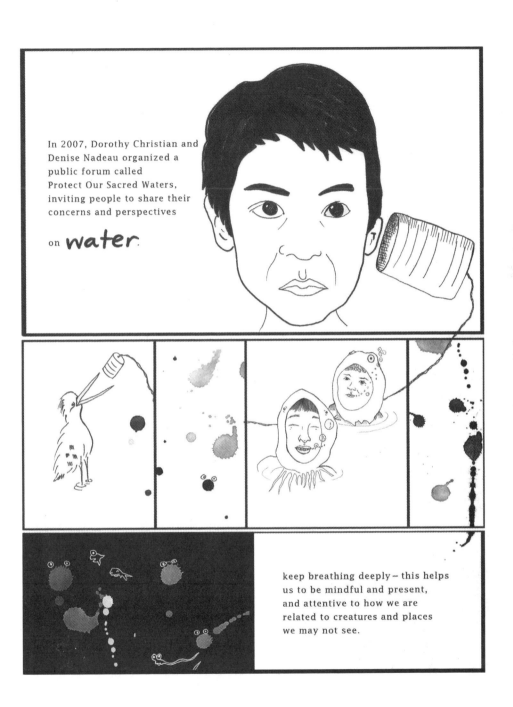

In 2007, Dorothy Christian and Denise Nadeau organized a public forum called Protect Our Sacred Waters, inviting people to share their concerns and perspectives

on water.

keep breathing deeply – this helps us to be mindful and present, and attentive to how we are related to creatures and places we may not see.

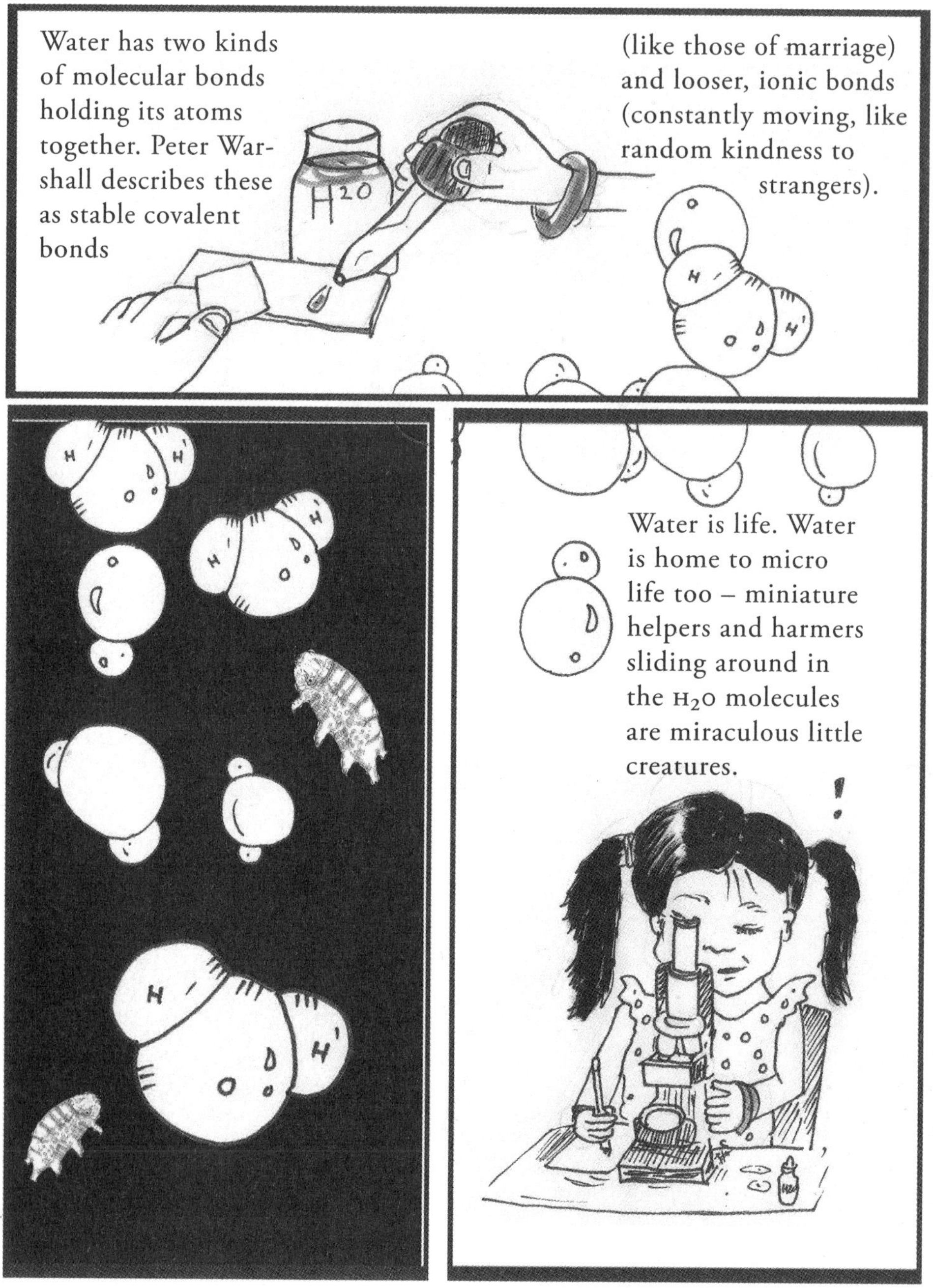
Water has two kinds of molecular bonds holding its atoms together. Peter Warshall describes these as stable covalent bonds
H2O
(like those of marriage) and looser, ionic bonds (constantly moving, like random kindness to strangers).
Water is life. Water is home to micro life too – miniature helpers and harmers sliding around in the H2O molecules are miraculous little creatures.
!

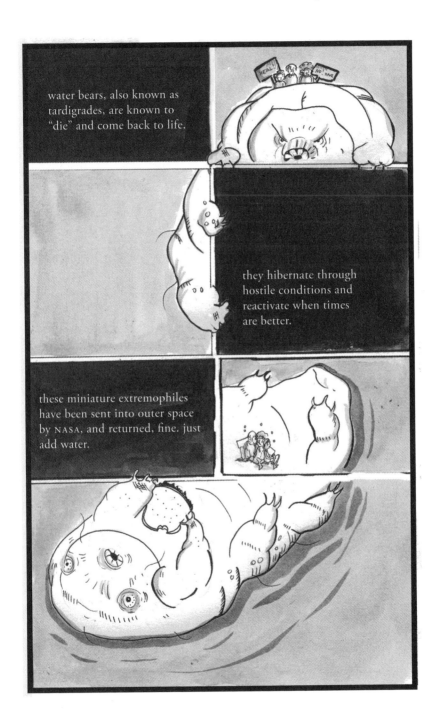

water bears, also known as tardigrades, are known to "die" and come back to life.

they hibernate through hostile conditions and reactivate when times are better.

these miniature extremophiles have been sent into outer space by NASA, and returned, fine. just add water.

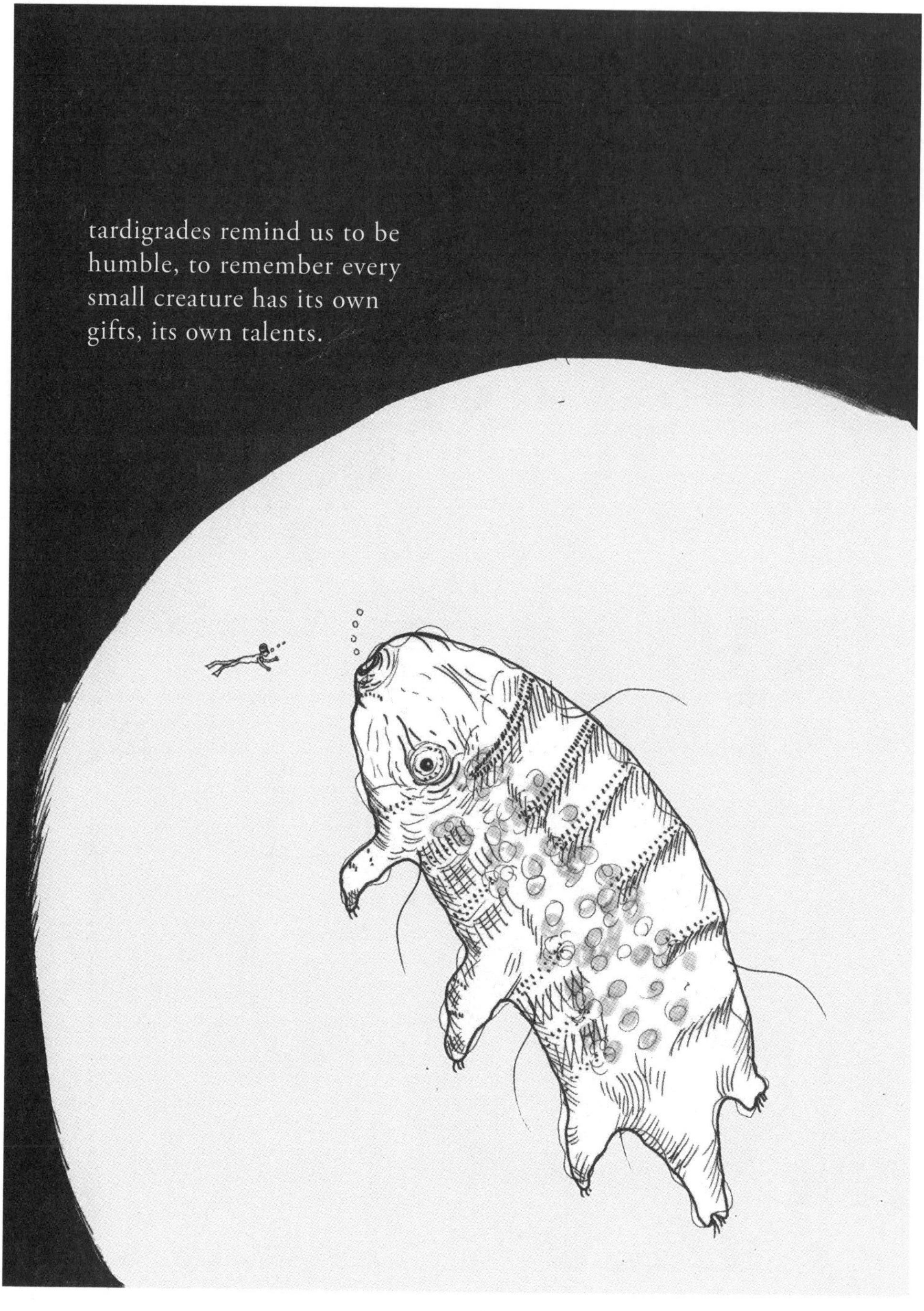
tardigrades remind us to be
humble, to remember every
small creature has its own
gifts, its own talents.

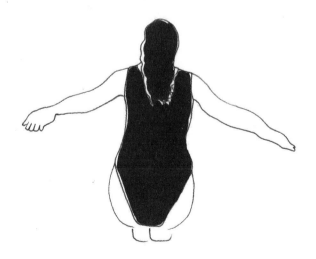

dragonfly dawning:
move in all directions you need

crimson-ringed whitefaces

deliberate dive

sedge sprites

balanced swoop

emerald spreadwings

graceful glide

blue dashers

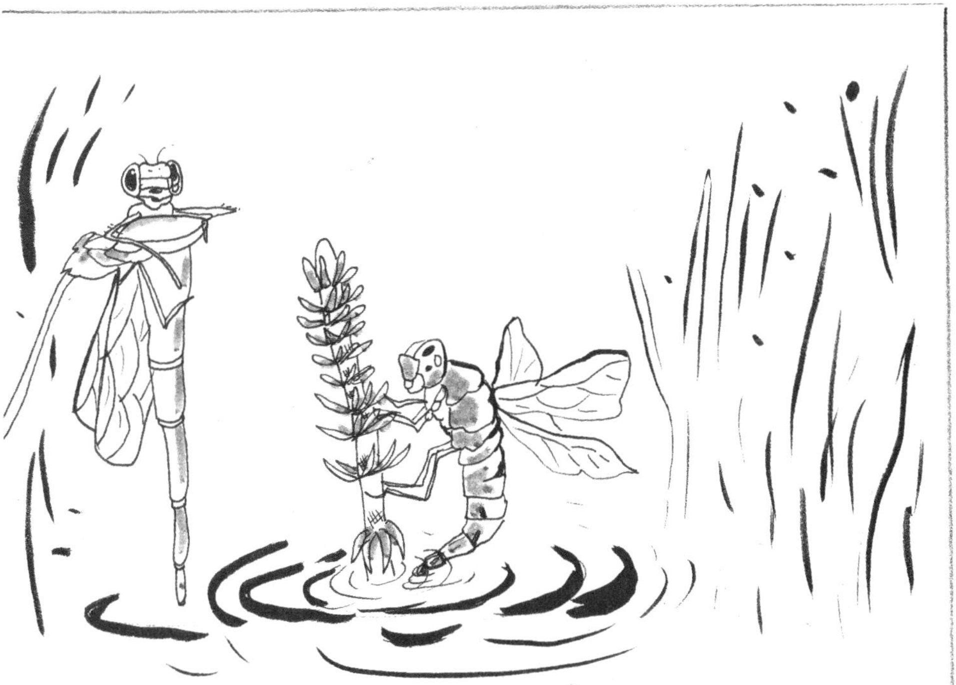

wizardly whoosh

saffron-winged meadowhawks

crepuscular climb

pond damsels

autonomously ascend

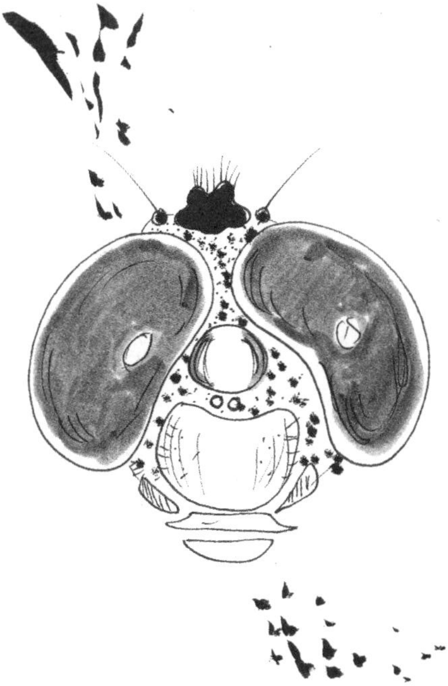

making pacific

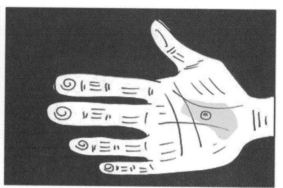

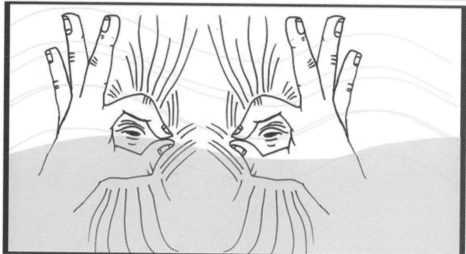

at its headwaters **staləw**
is translucent jade,
clean and delicious

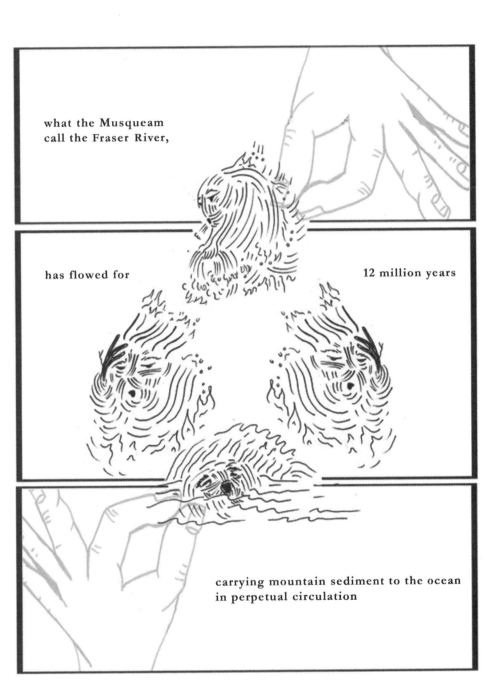

what the Musqueam
call the Fraser River,

has flowed for

12 million years

carrying mountain sediment to the ocean
in perpetual circulation

the river is a 12-million-year-old elder...

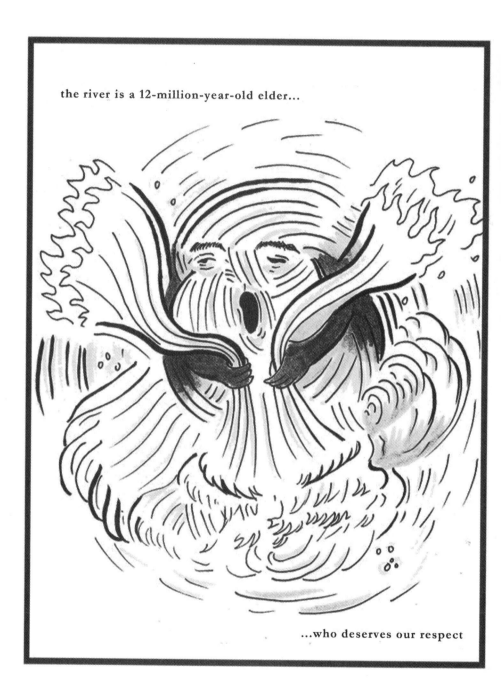

...who deserves our respect

it's been said that
future wars will be fought
over water in the way they
are fought over oil
today

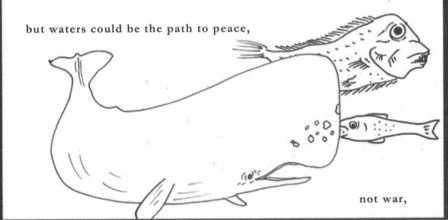

but waters could be the path to peace,

not war,

if we have the vision and the commitment.
waters offer an opportunity and
a requirement to work together to respect
them, and in doing so, respect ourselves.

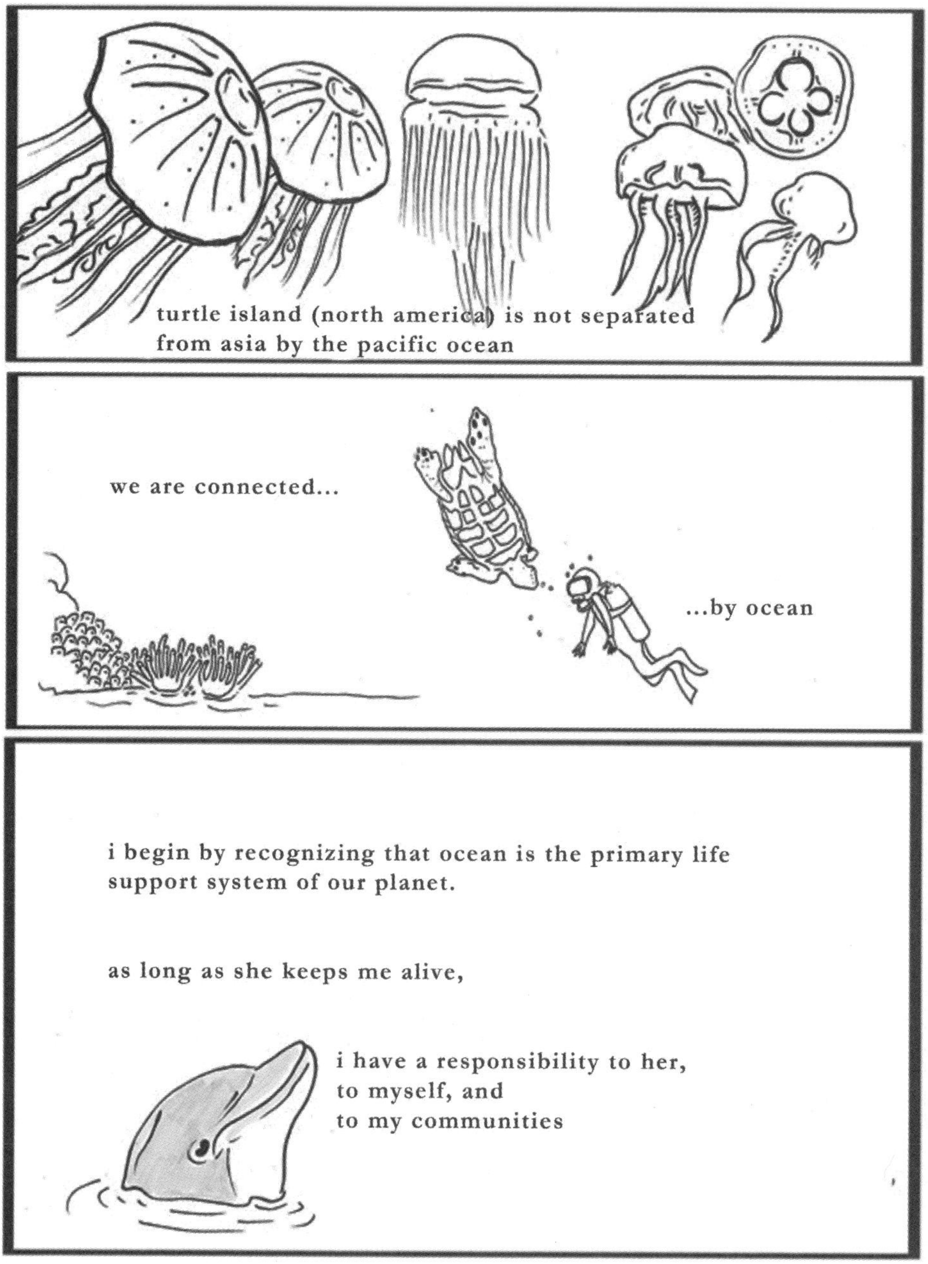
turtle island (north america) is not separated
from asia by the pacific ocean
we are connected...
...by ocean
i begin by recognizing that ocean is the primary life
support system of our planet.
as long as she keeps me alive,
i have a responsibility to her,
to myself, and
to my communities

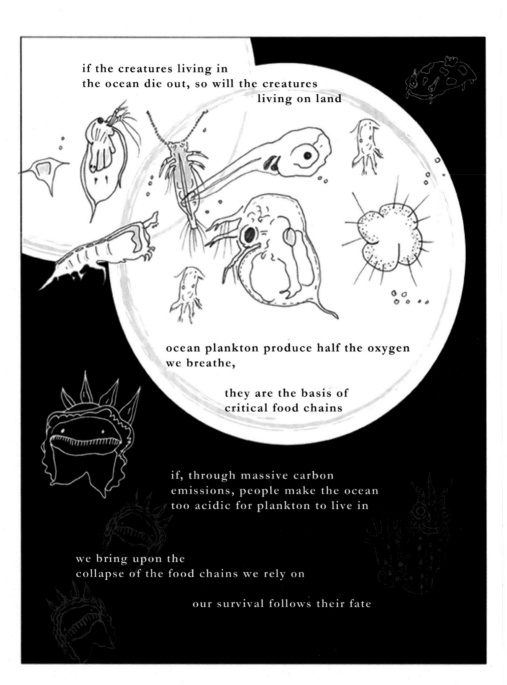

if the creatures living in
the ocean die out, so will the creatures
living on land

ocean plankton produce half the oxygen
we breathe,

they are the basis of
critical food chains

if, through massive carbon
emissions, people make the ocean
too acidic for plankton to live in

we bring upon the
collapse of the food chains we rely on

our survival follows their fate

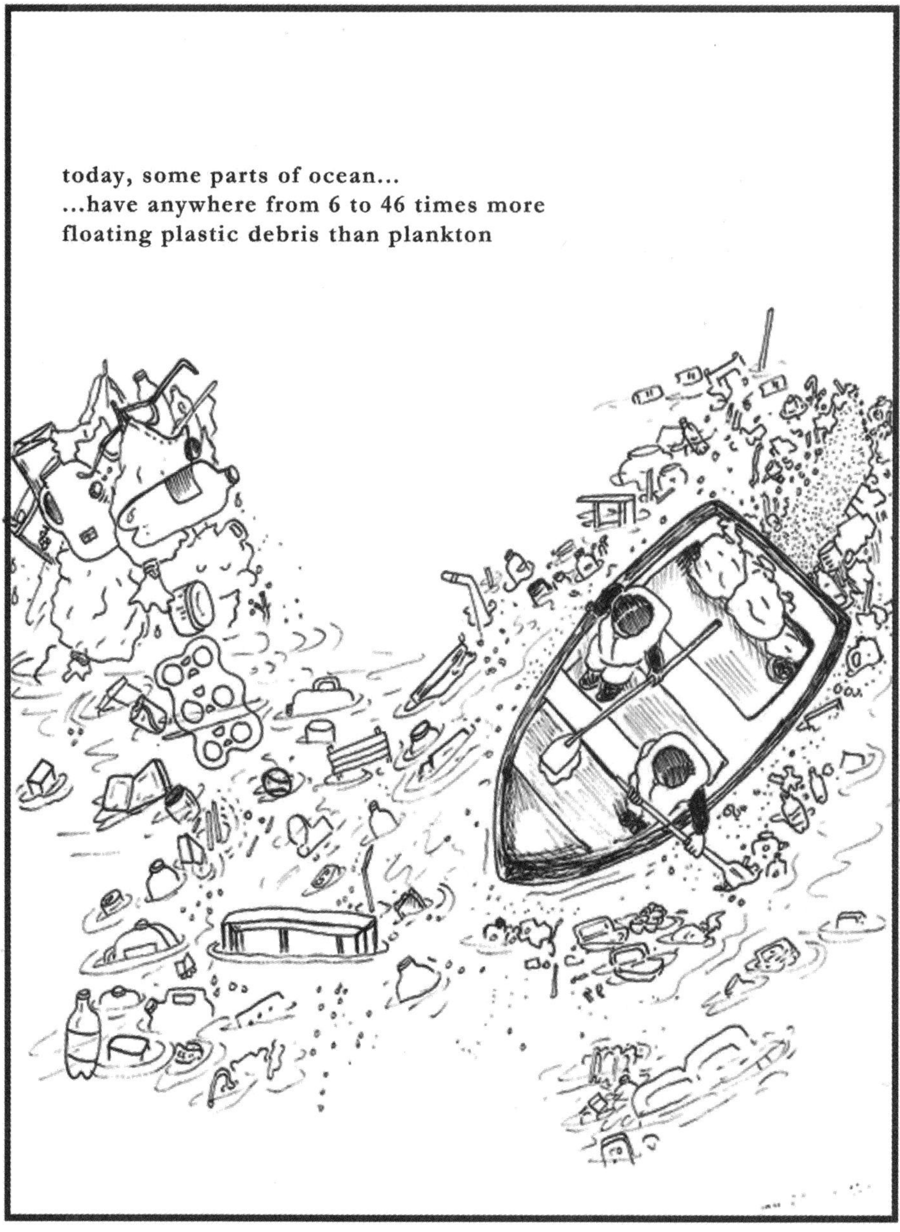
today, some parts of ocean...
...have anywhere from 6 to 46 times more floating plastic debris than plankton

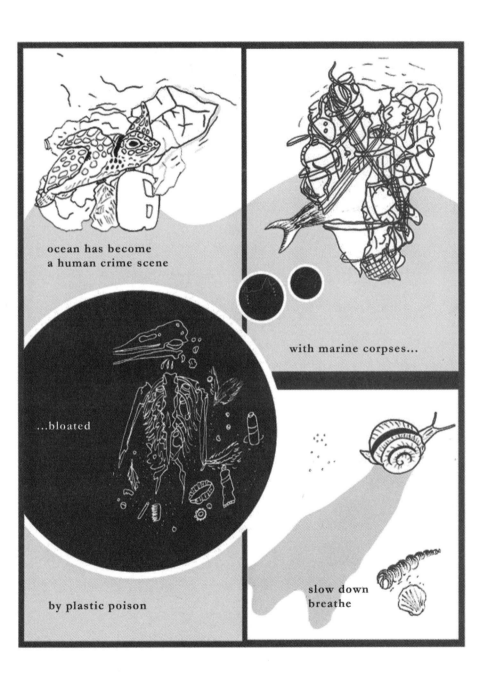

ocean has become
a human crime scene

with marine corpses...

...bloated

by plastic poison

slow down
breathe

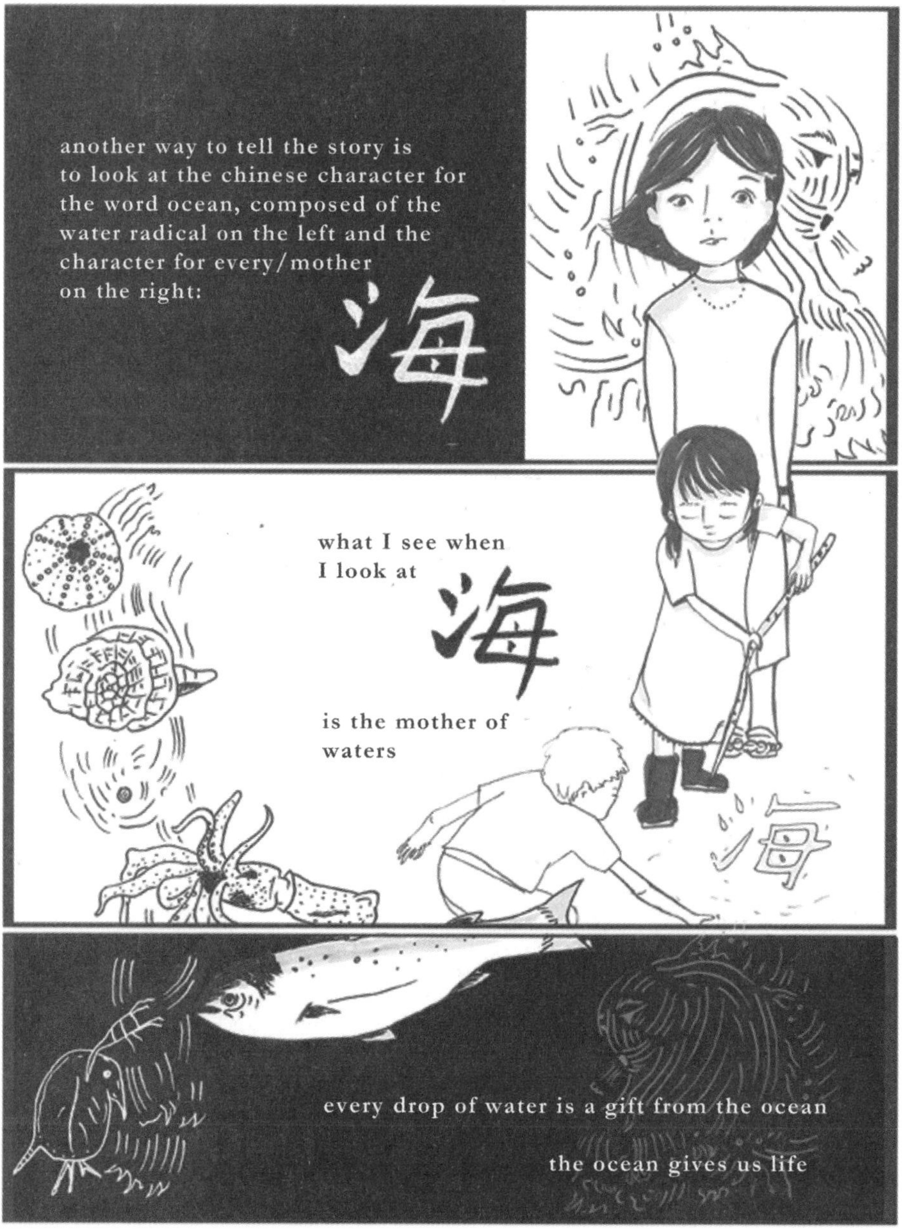
another way to tell the story is
to look at the chinese character for
the word ocean, composed of the
water radical on the left and the
character for every/mother
on the right:
海
what I see when
I look at
海
is the mother of
waters
海
every drop of water is a gift from the ocean
the ocean gives us life

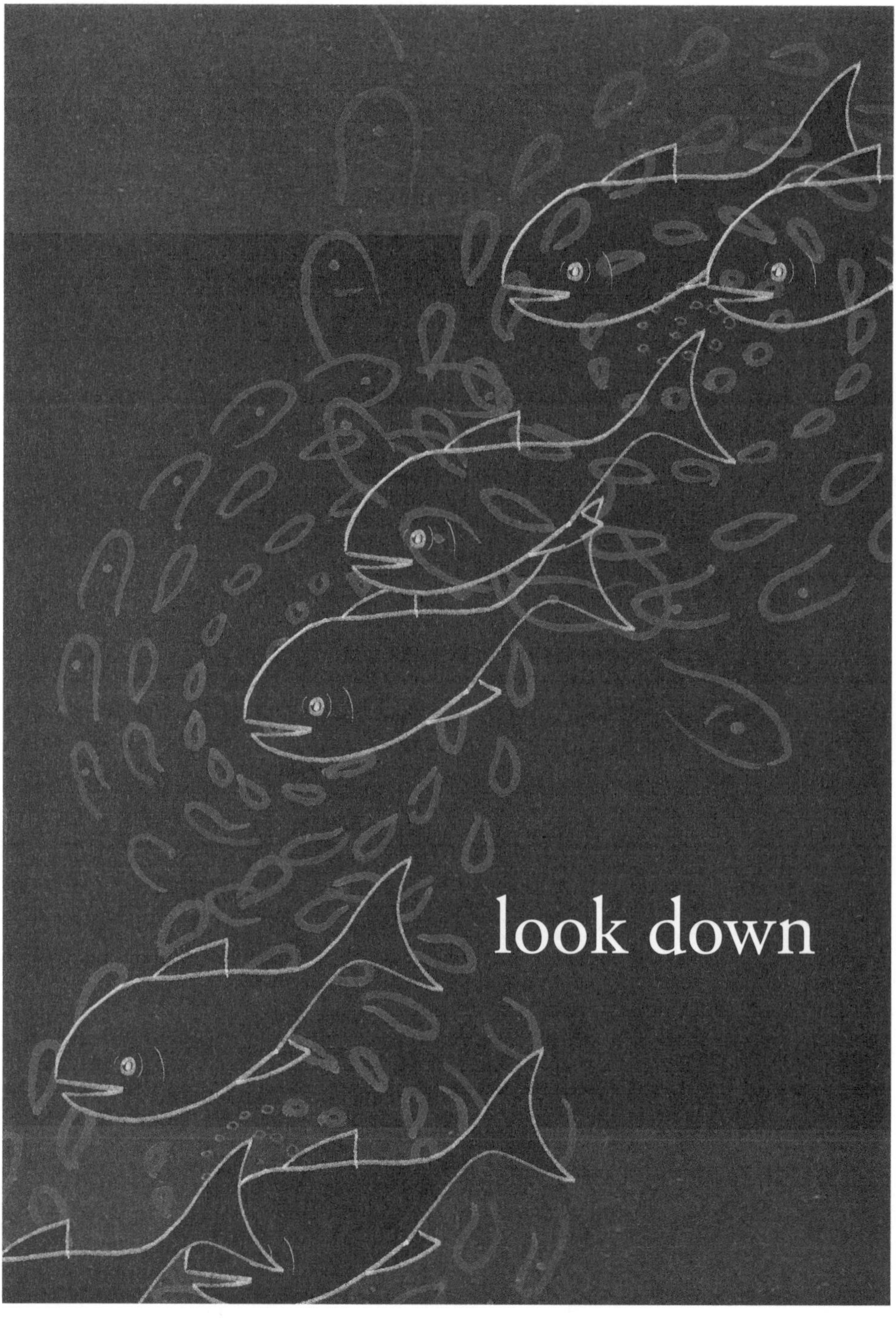
look down

non-productive   or not precious enough   glacial
deposit
banked moraine   fire hydrant
Coney Island whitefish
   purple thistle   bamboo   bus shelter
                       shadow
hollowed boulder   rich guano   long-
needled pine
   porch shade   a child's dropped shoe

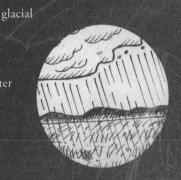

                    glistening slug trail
                    bramble   unseen cricket
                    ant excavation dust
                       tsunami debris dust   crow feather
                       twig rustle
                             sun-dried gum blob   sidewalk crack
                    dioxin dust
                    broken glass   frayed wire
                    leaf litter
                       phthalate dust   cigarette butt   bottle cap
                    copper penny   plastic wrap   straw
                       out of balance
                    cracked plastic bottle   tin foil moth
                    corpse

road kill   pollen   ziplocked bags
tissue decay   crushed pebble   lost pen
   dropped sock   barbed wire   cracked tube
worn concrete   faded wrapper   orphaned lid
   faint stencil   eroded elastic   ticket stub
          styrofoam cup   crushed canvas   shredded
tire
loosened bandaid   flattened glove   sawdust

      paint smudge   rust stain burger wrapper
crap to carnage   capital to carnival
   crumpled twist-tie   broken ruler   ragged newspaper
   oil-smeared plate   weathered gravel   PVC chip
crinkly cellophane   ceramic shard
dung

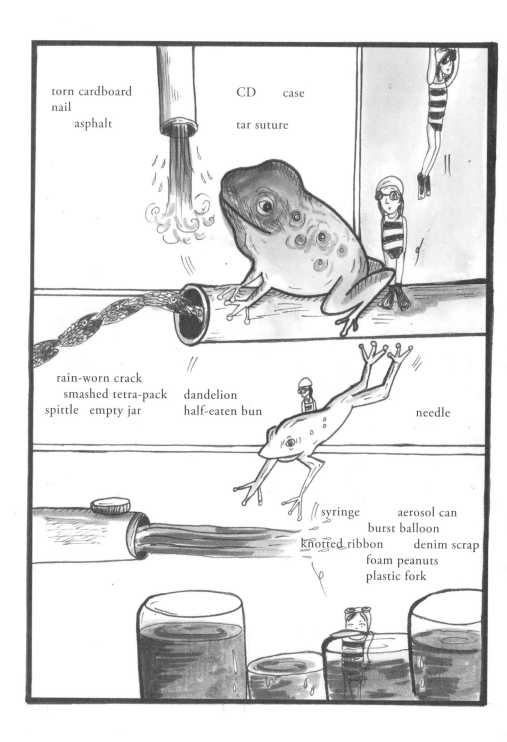

torn cardboard
nail
    asphalt

CD   case

tar suture

rain-worn crack
    smashed tetra-pack   dandelion
spittle empty jar   half-eaten bun

needle

syringe   aerosol can
    burst balloon
knotted ribbon   denim scrap
    foam peanuts
    plastic fork

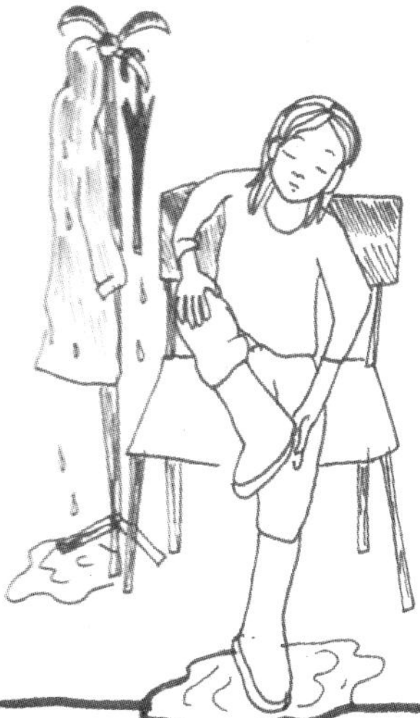

rotted apple aluminum pull tab
lollipop wrapper shopping bag baggage tag
bus transfer aspirin bottle ladybug
worm corpse juice carton
torn receipt

– observed on a short East Van bike ride

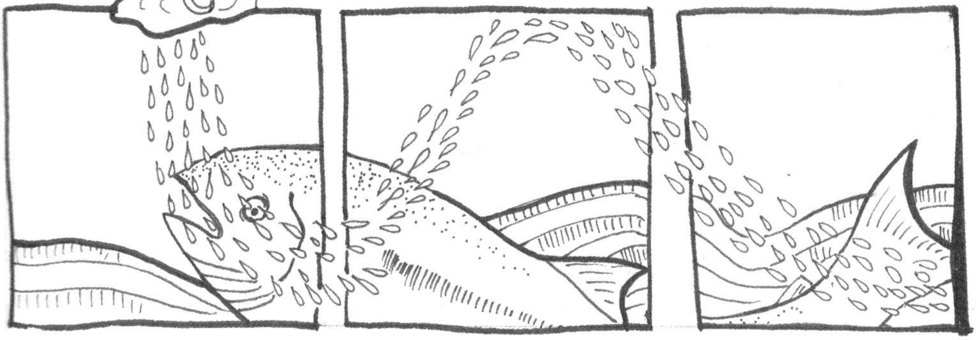

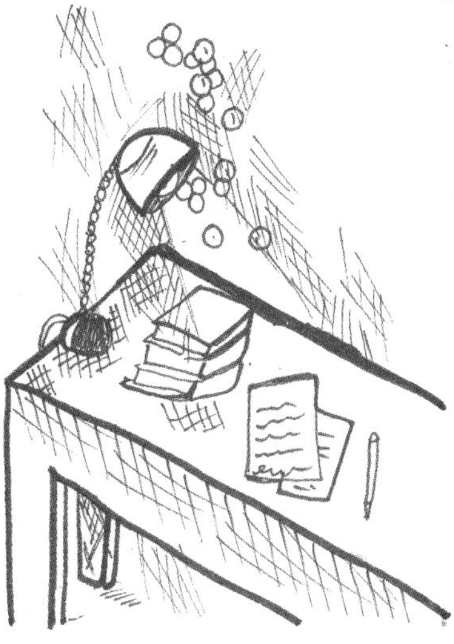

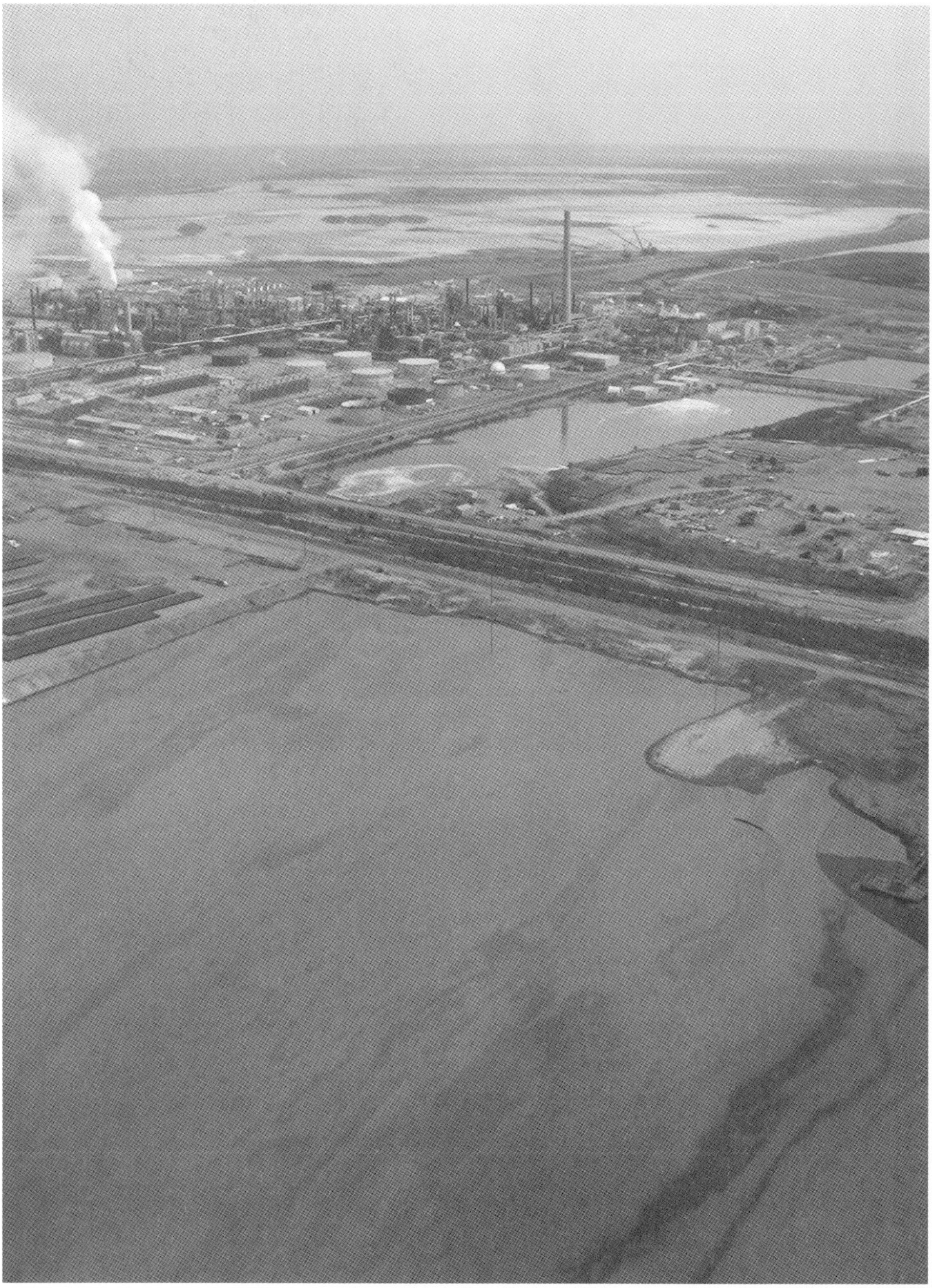

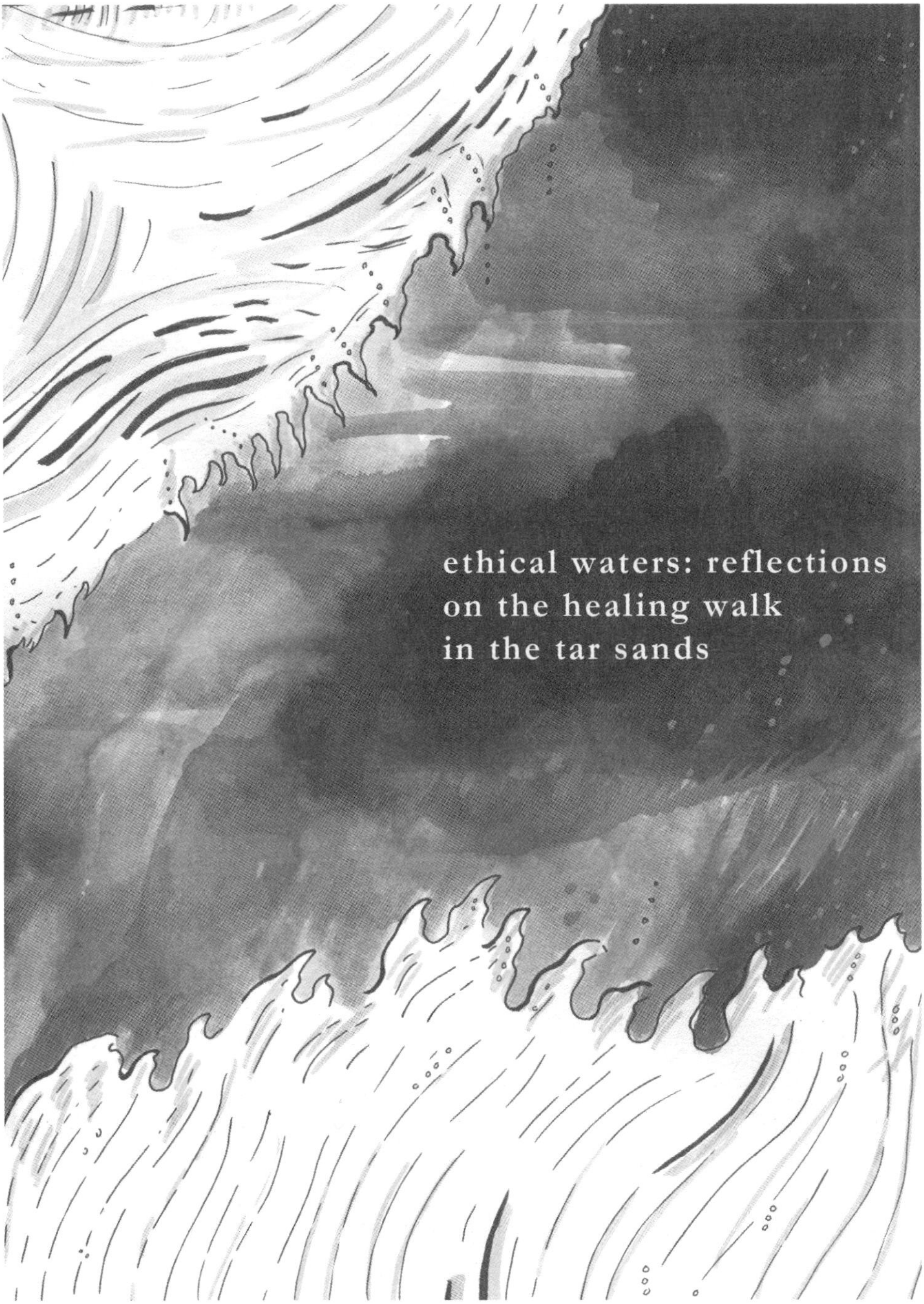

ethical waters: reflections on the healing walk in the tar sands

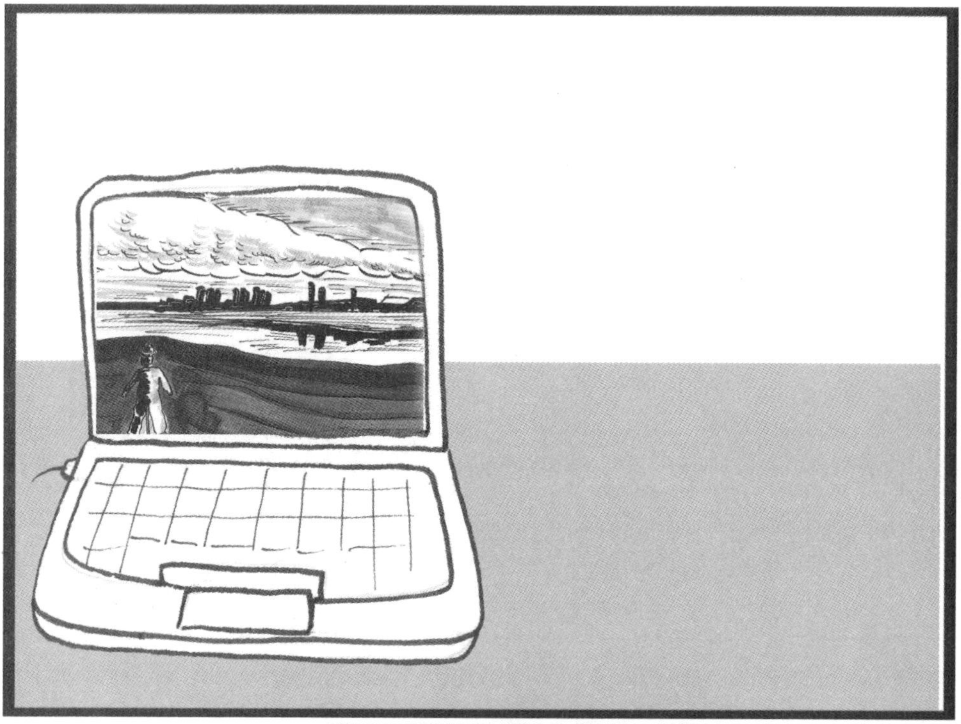

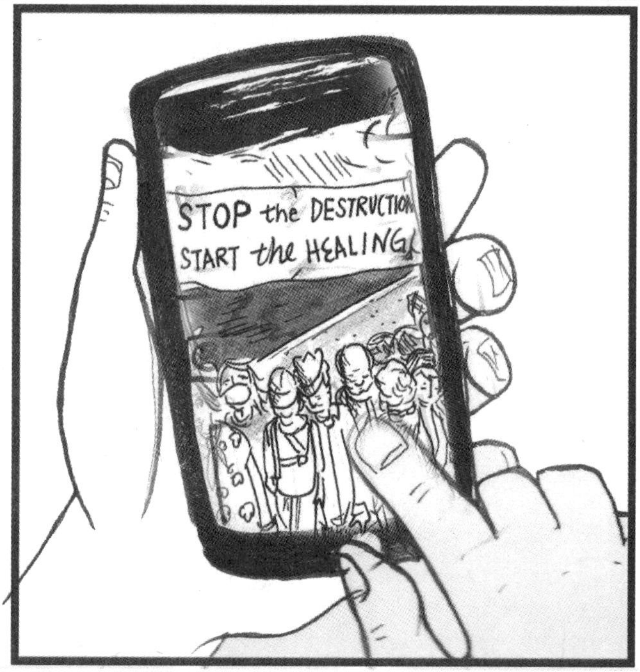
STOP the DESTRUCTION
START the HEALING

(held hostage by injustice)

how do you respond to...

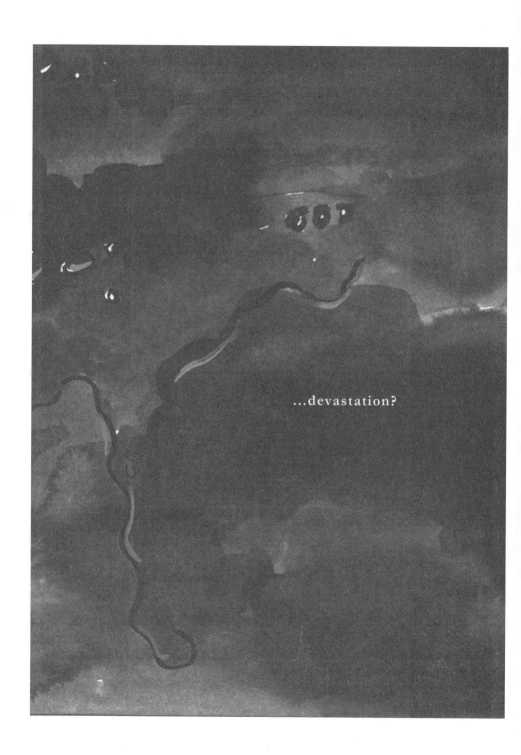

...devastation?

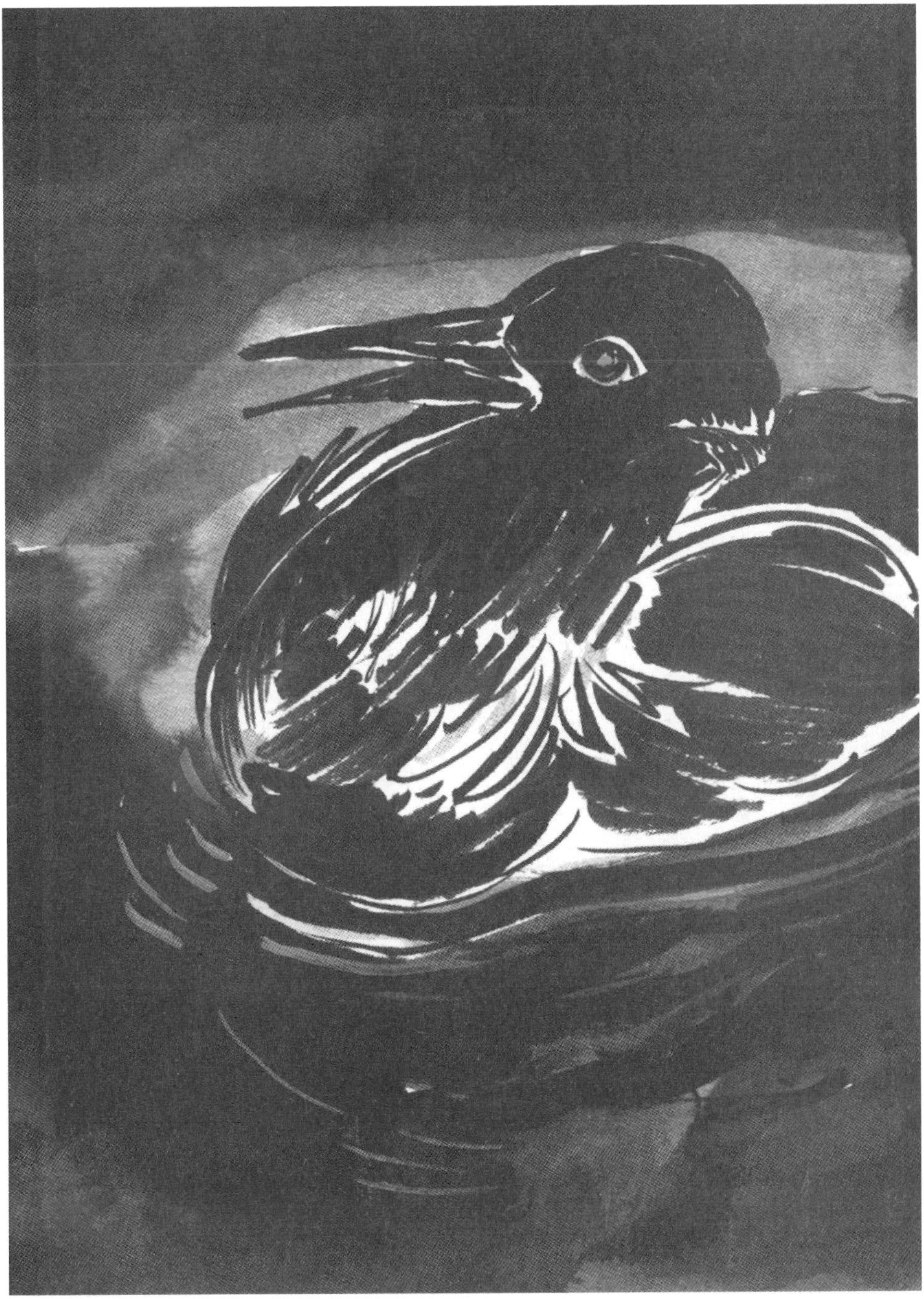

alone & small, you look & listen for others

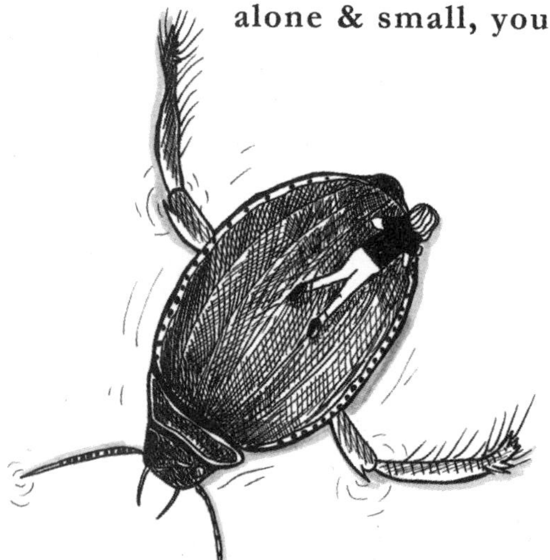

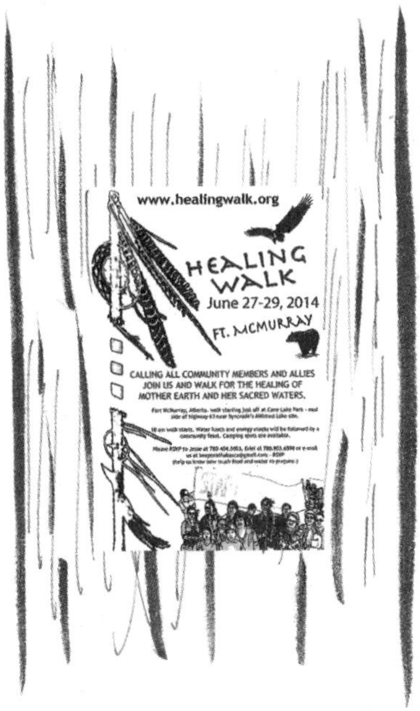
www.healingwalk.org
HEALING WALK
June 27-29, 2014
FT. MCMURRAY
CALLING ALL COMMUNITY MEMBERS AND ALLIES
JOIN US AND WALK FOR THE HEALING OF
MOTHER EARTH AND HER SACRED WATERS.

you hear a call for healing from
Indigenous peoples and friends

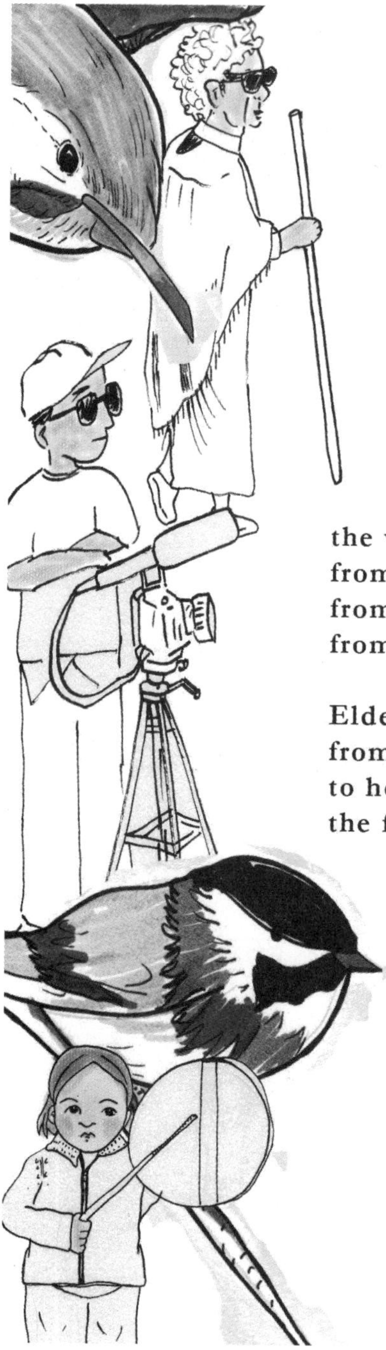

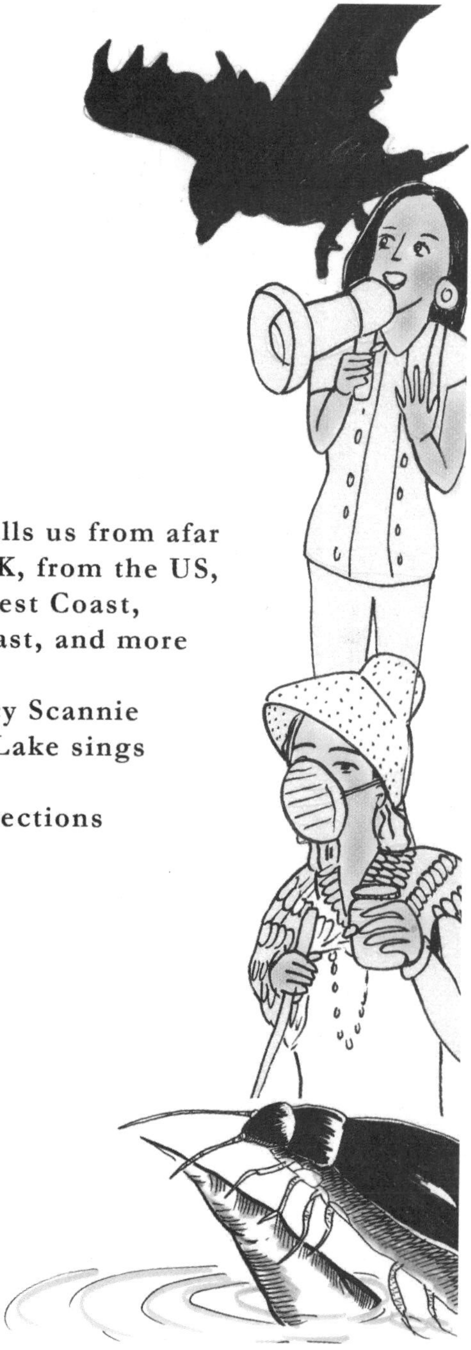

the walk calls us from afar
from the UK, from the US,
from the West Coast,
from the East, and more

Elder Nancy Scannie
from Cold Lake sings
to honour
the four directions

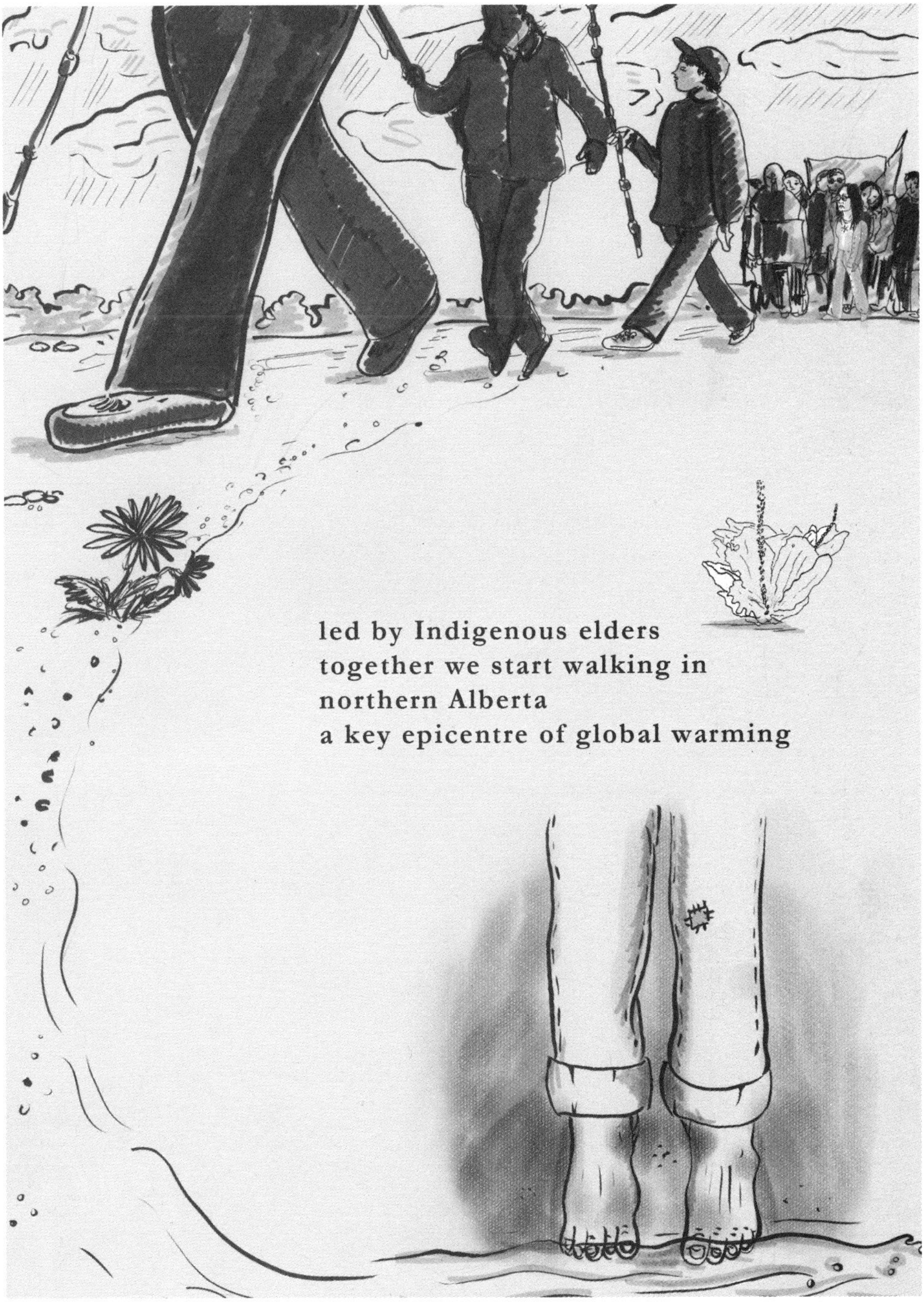

led by Indigenous elders
together we start walking in
northern Alberta
a key epicentre of global warming

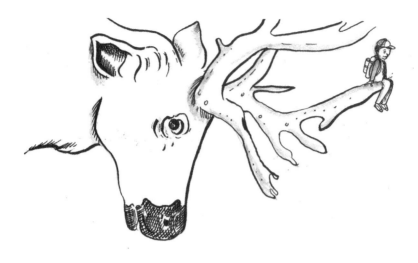

we walk for the caribou

that the Athabasca Chipewyan First Nation
is trying to protect

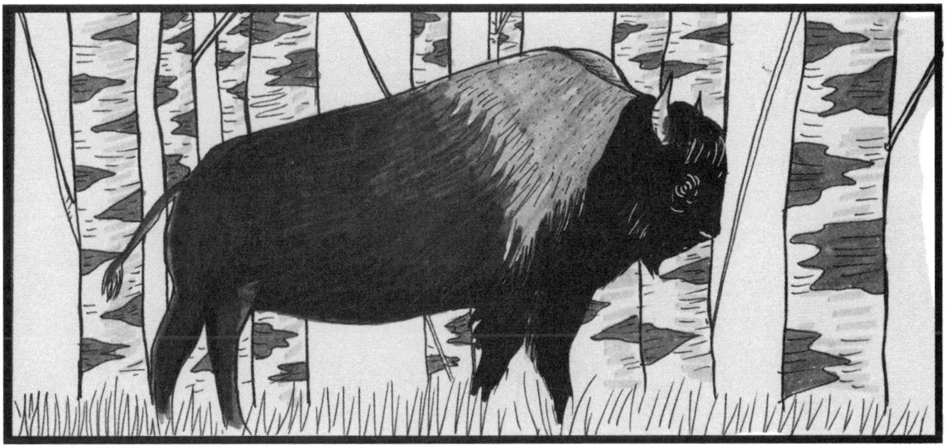

the thunzea (woodland caribou),
et'thén (barren ground caribou),
dechen yághe ejere (wood bison),
and more

peaceful and humble

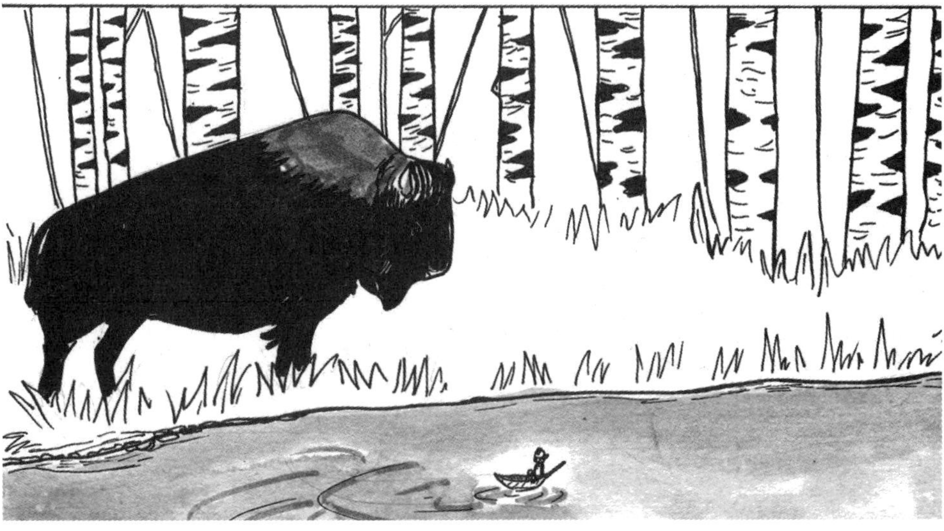

George Poitras of the Mikisew Cree
asks for a moment
of silence to pay respect to the people in Fort Chipewyan
and Fort McMurray who've died of cancer

Elder Violet Cheechum Clarke says:
"We always had running water.
We always had light."

before rapid expansion of
the oil industry,
her community lived in
sustainable balance,
drinking water straight
from the rivers
and living by sunlight

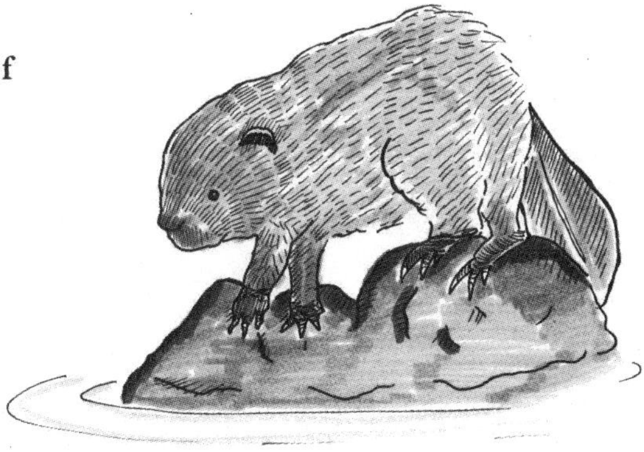

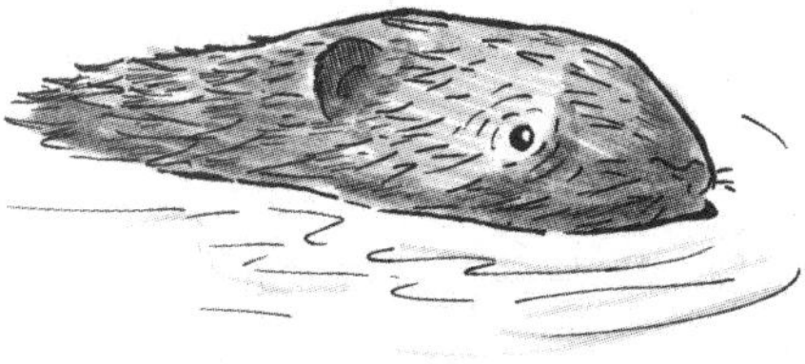

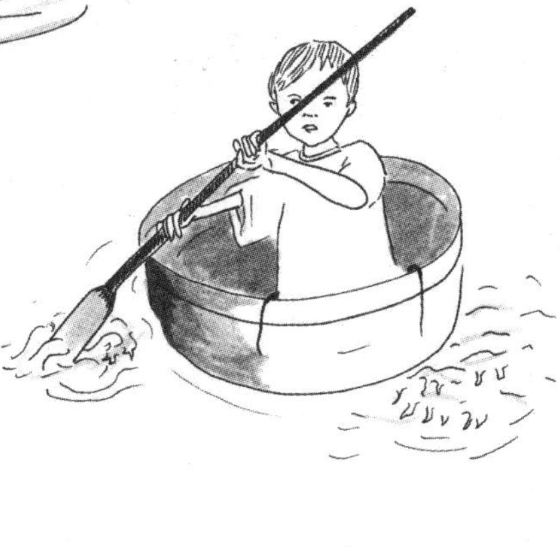

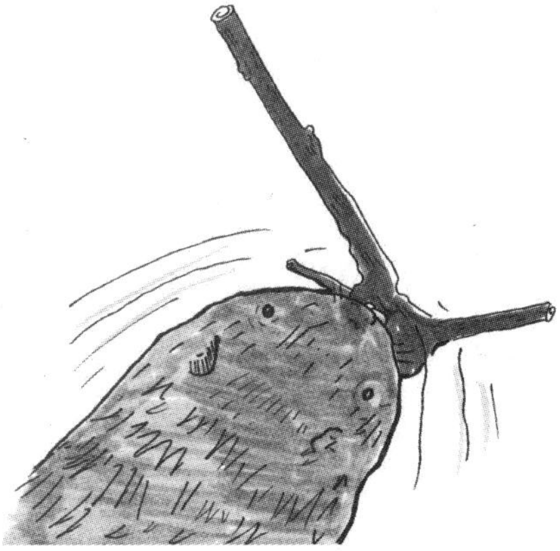

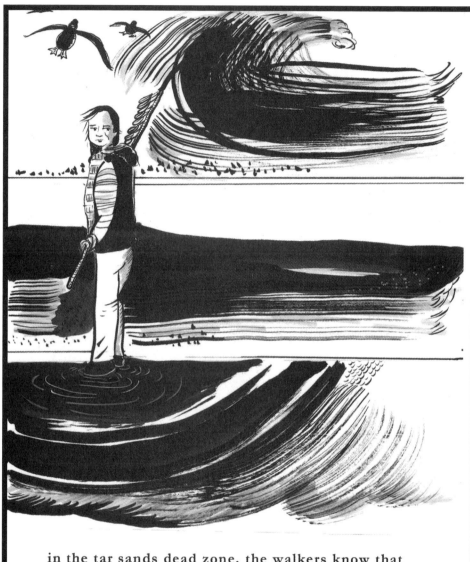

in the tar sands dead zone, the walkers know that
a paradigm shift is urgently needed to cool down
the planet's industrially induced fever.
this shift is already here—honest, practical and strong
in spirit.

living in the belly of the
bitumen beast
driving and flying,
i am implicated in
the oil addiction
that i critique.

my hands are reluctantly dirty, black with oil
and tar. but this is the first step in a journey of recovery
for an addict to move to renewable energies

"Another world is not only possible, she is on her way."

—Arundhati Roy

change is inevitable

the question is what kind of changes we make for
future generations

walking through the desecration, we reconnect with
the spirit of the land, the water, the living creatures

we assert our love
we don't give up
healing is needed
the earth will heal, with or without us

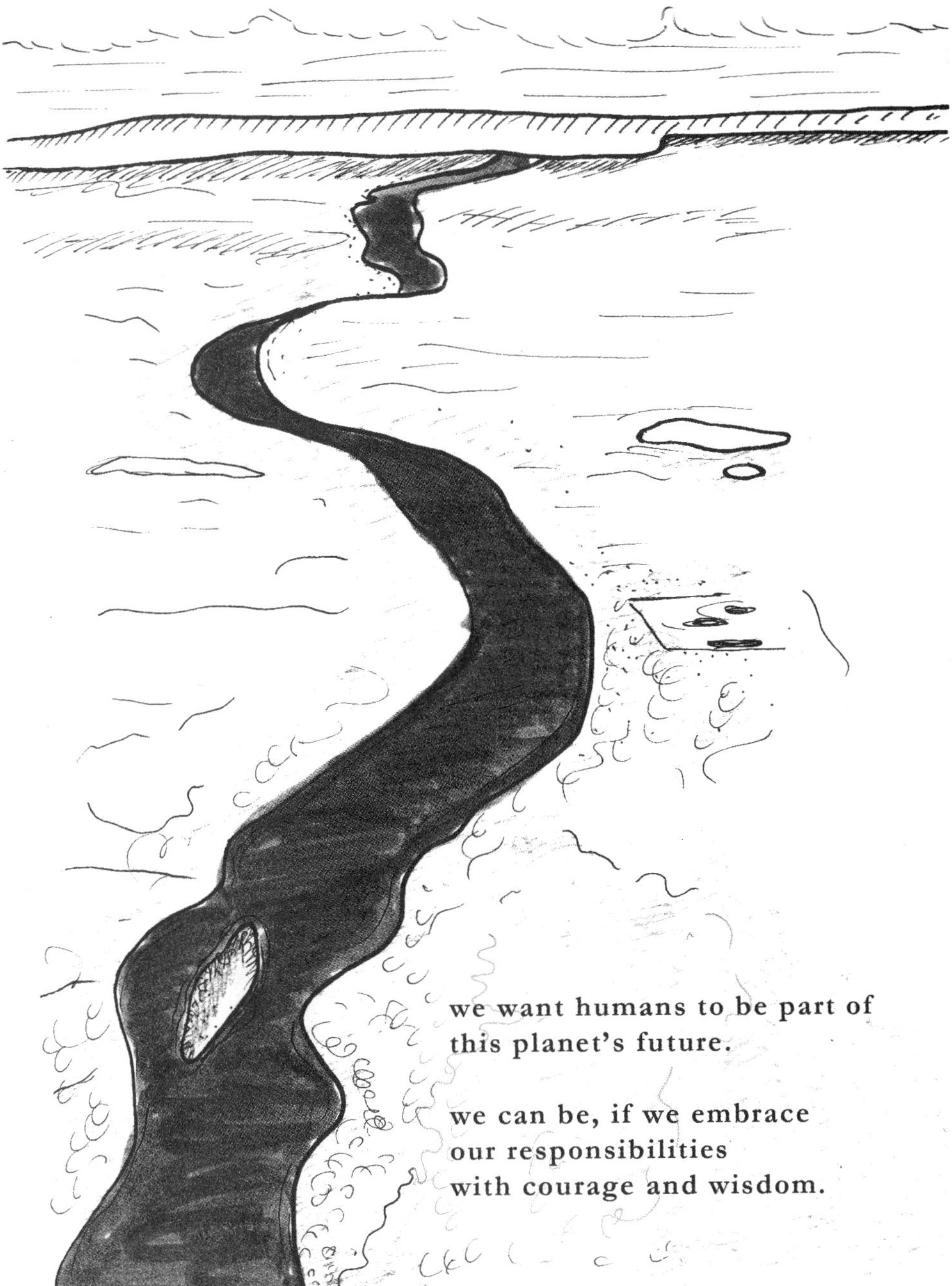

we want humans to be part of
this planet's future.

we can be, if we embrace
our responsibilities
with courage and wisdom.

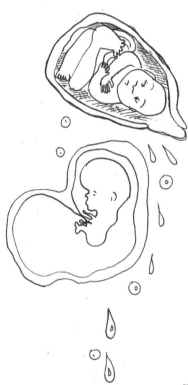

resurgence*

women take back their childbirth rituals
have freedom babies born from water**
reconnecting to land sparks life

*Found poem from "Land Is Life: Indigenous Defenders
Speak," December 2013. Italicized words are by Mel Bazil.
Gratitude to Mel, Kanahus Pelkey,** the Unist'ot'en clan,
and all the inspiring speakers that evening.

what can you do?

educate yourself,
educate others

everything you can do
talk, write, organize
ready for the battle
get out there on the land, with respect
walk barefoot on the earth, do it
stay connected to your own histories, cultures
& peoples
get ready for the next world

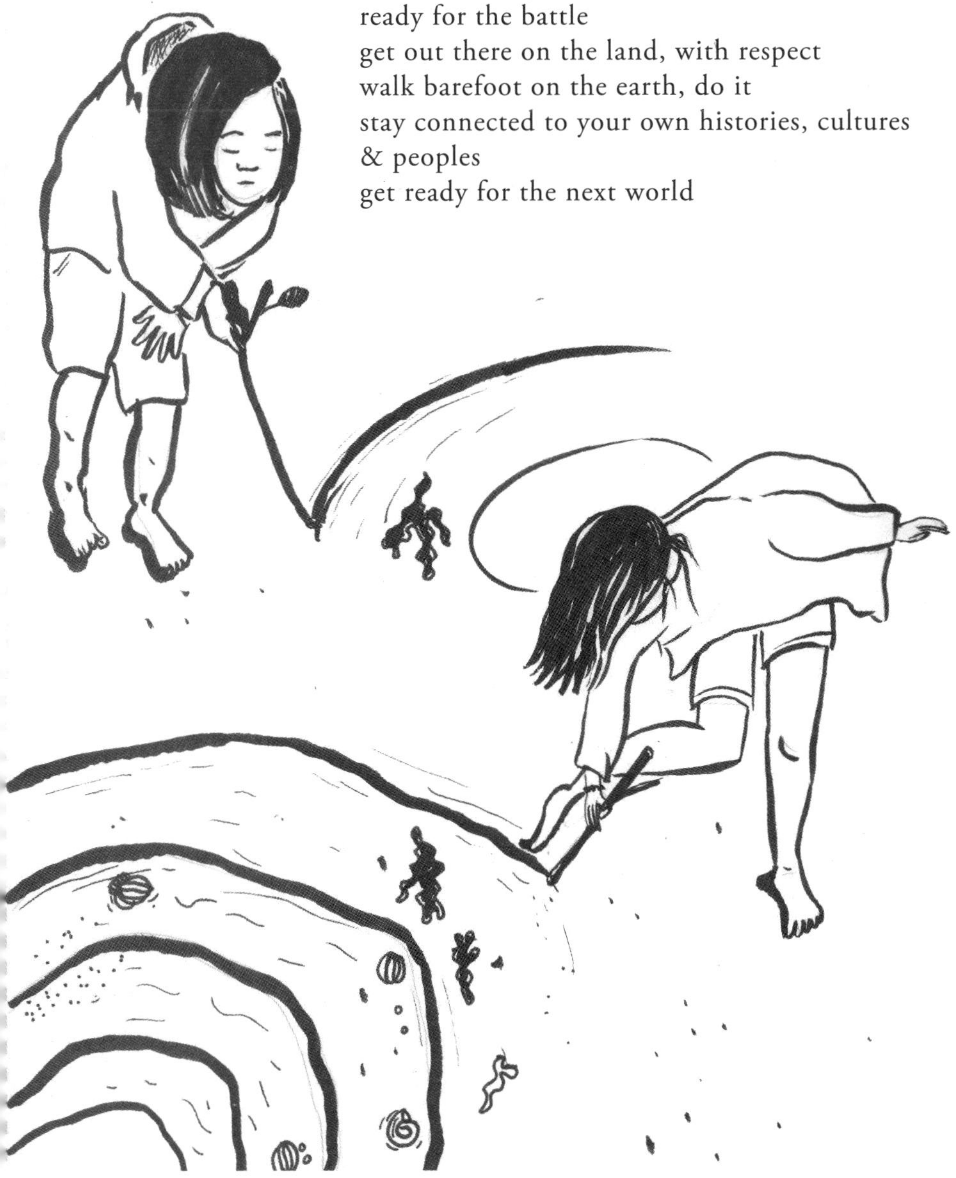

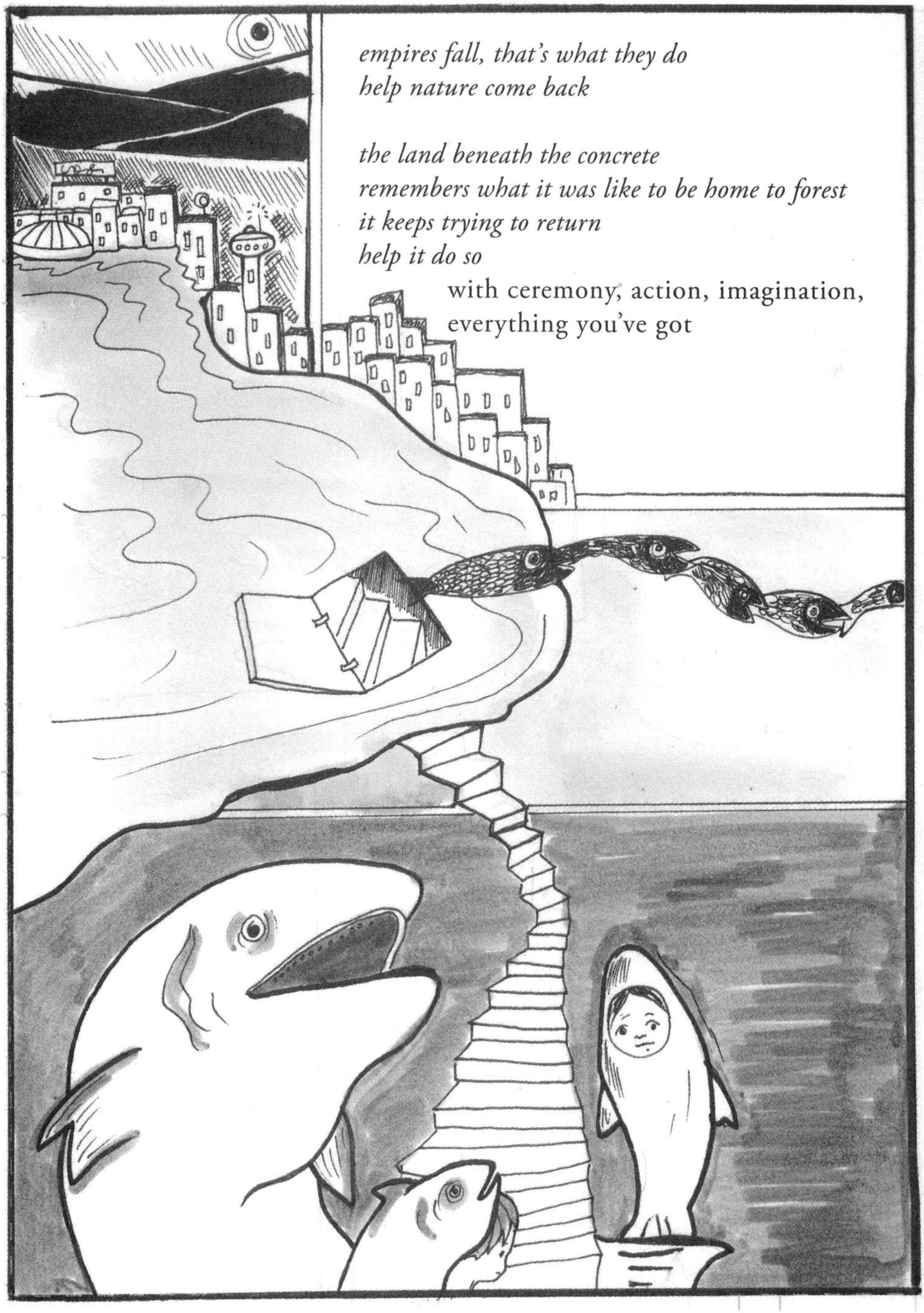
empires fall, that's what they do
help nature come back
the land beneath the concrete
remembers what it was like to be home to forest
it keeps trying to return
help it do so
with ceremony, action, imagination,
everything you've got

http://paddleforthepeace.ca/

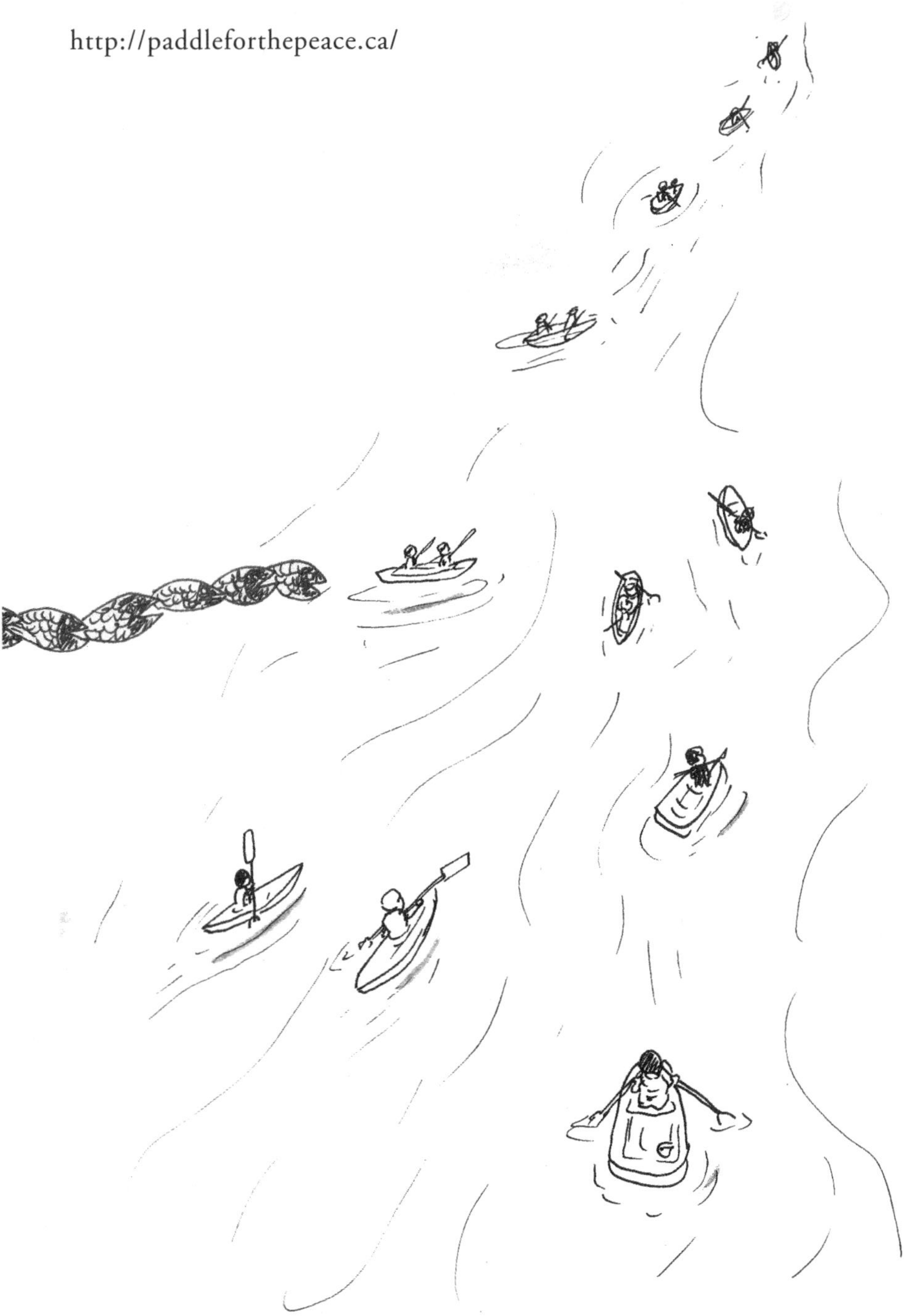

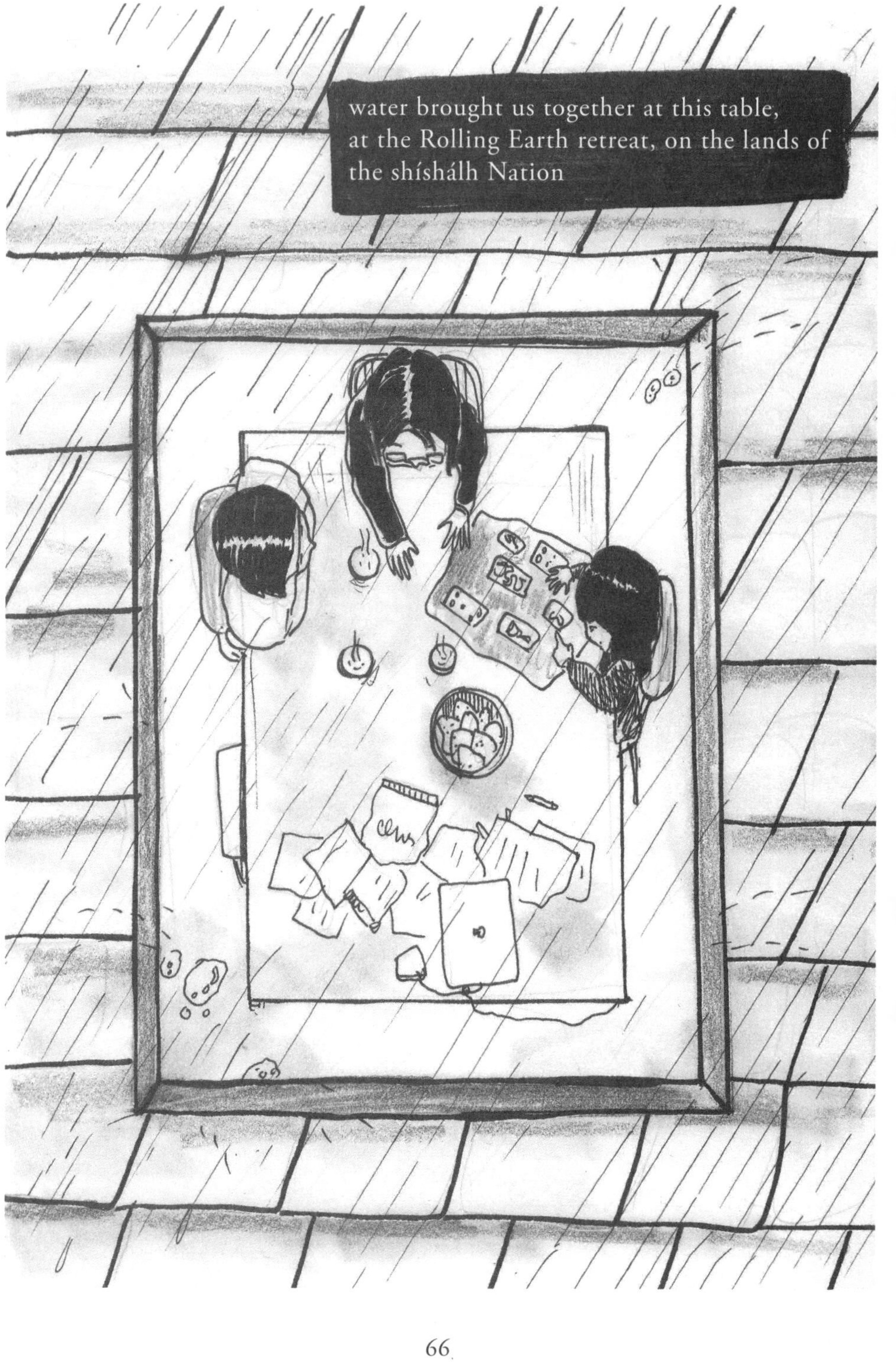
water brought us together at this table, at the Rolling Earth retreat, on the lands of the shíshálh Nation

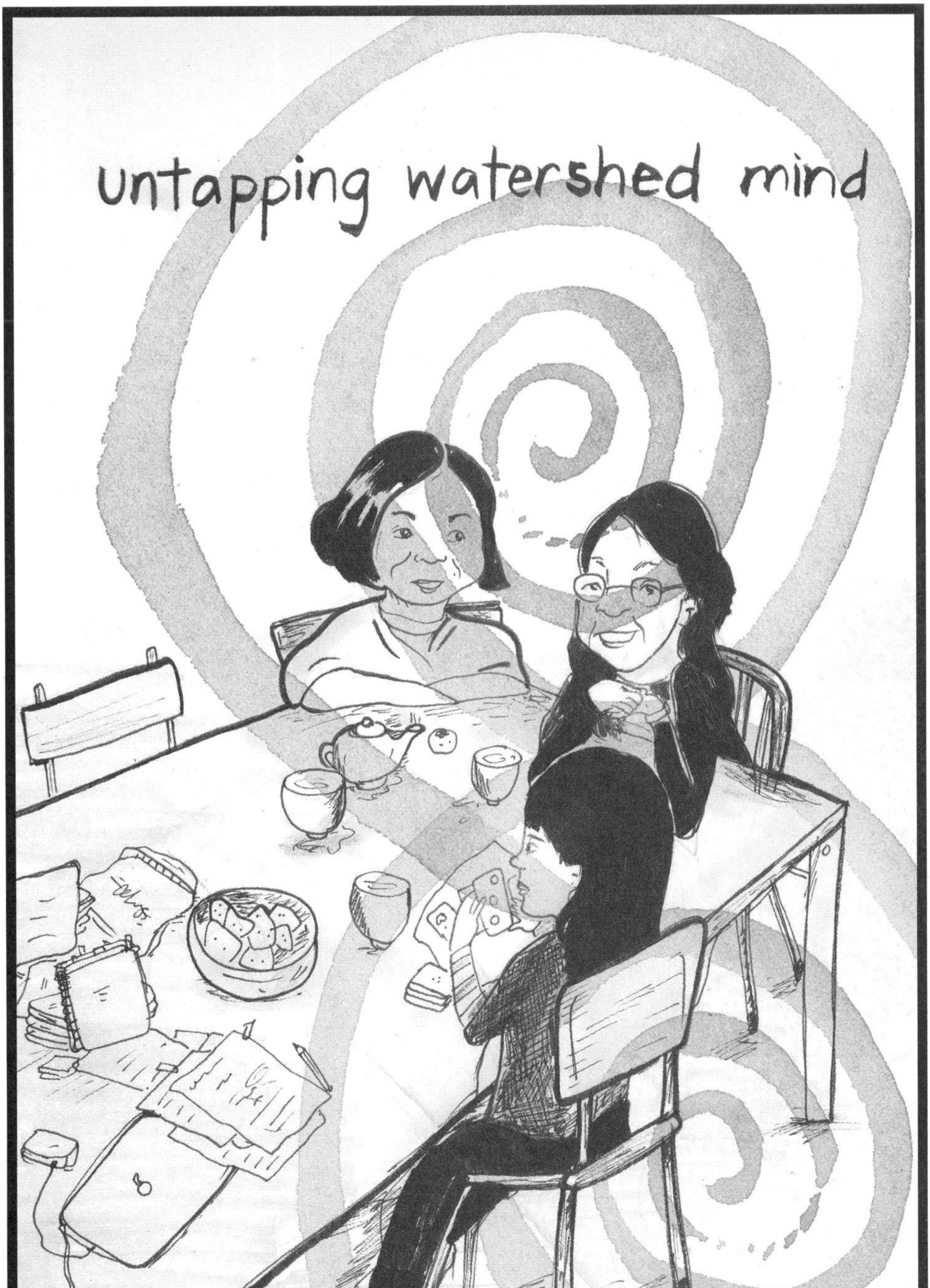
untapping watershed mind

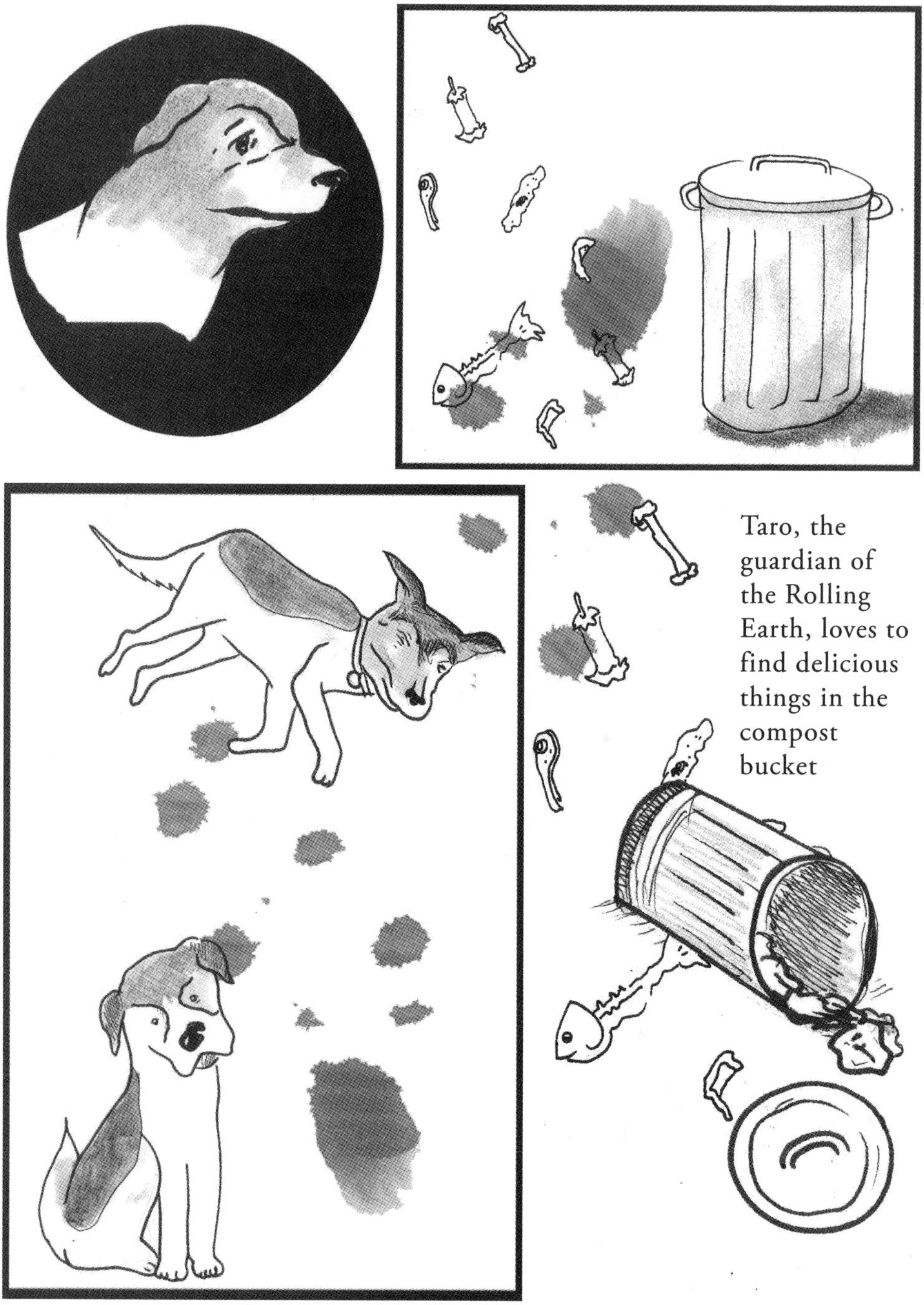
Taro, the guardian of the Rolling Earth, loves to find delicious things in the compost bucket

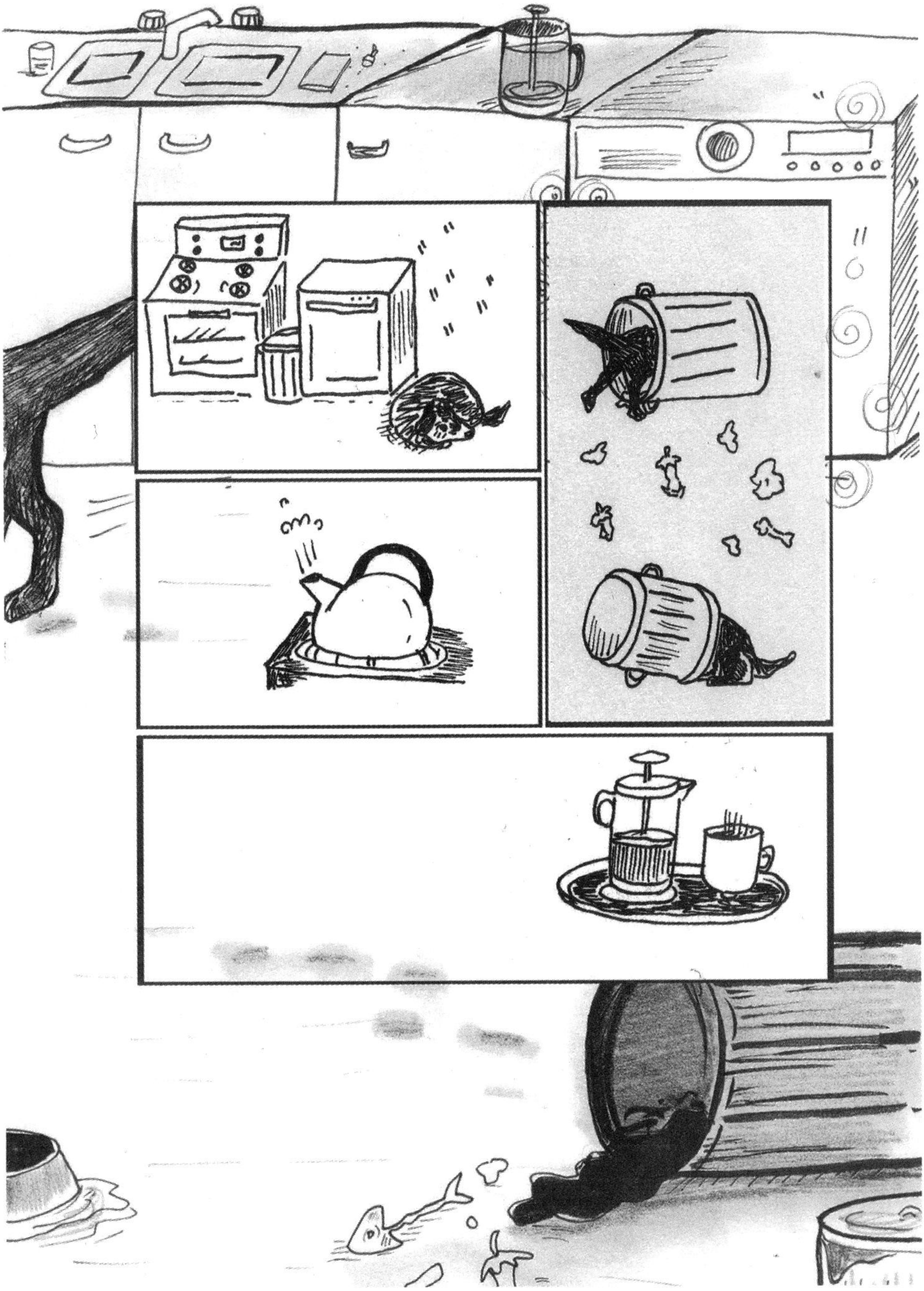

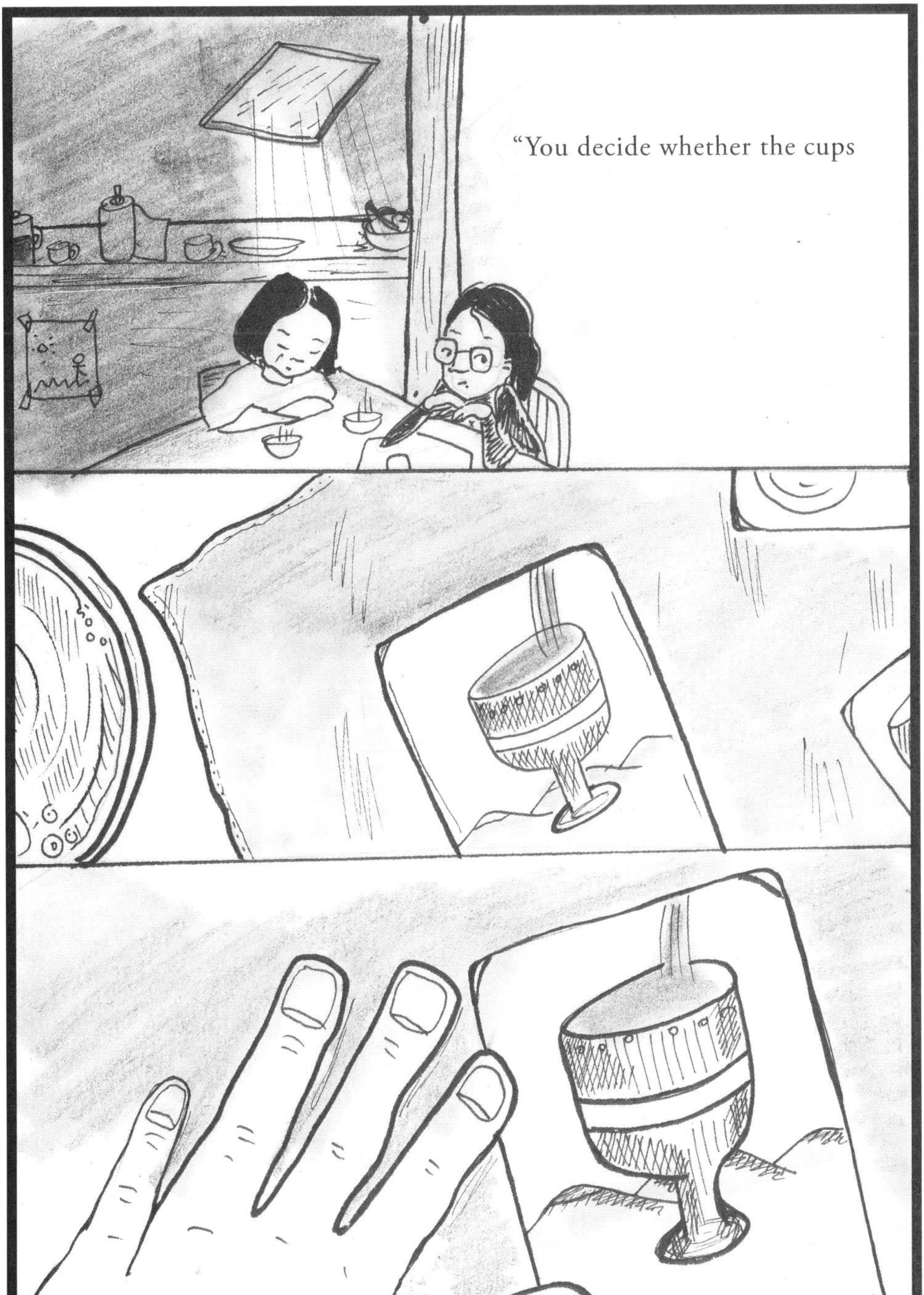
"You decide whether the cups

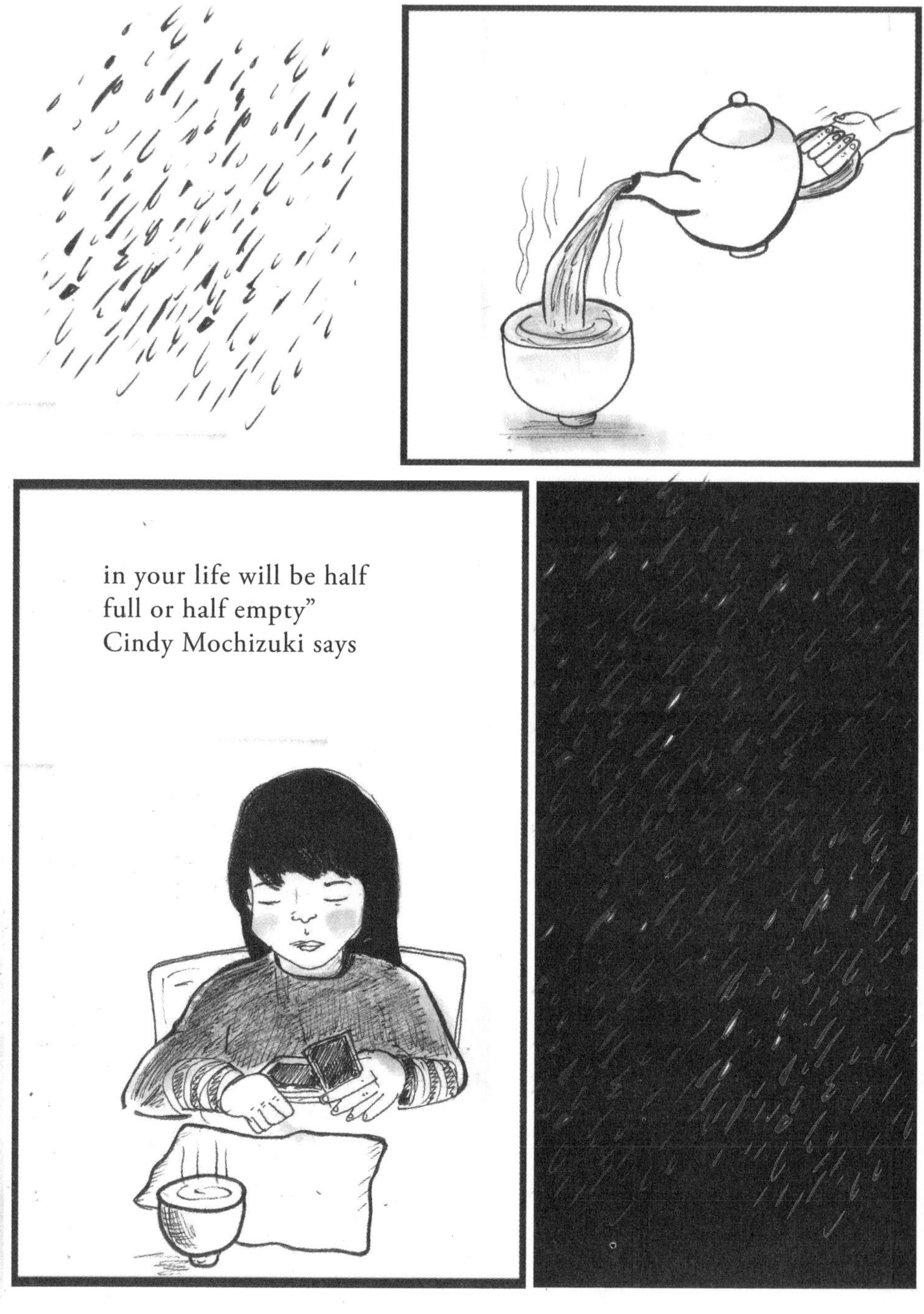
in your life will be half
full or half empty"
Cindy Mochizuki says

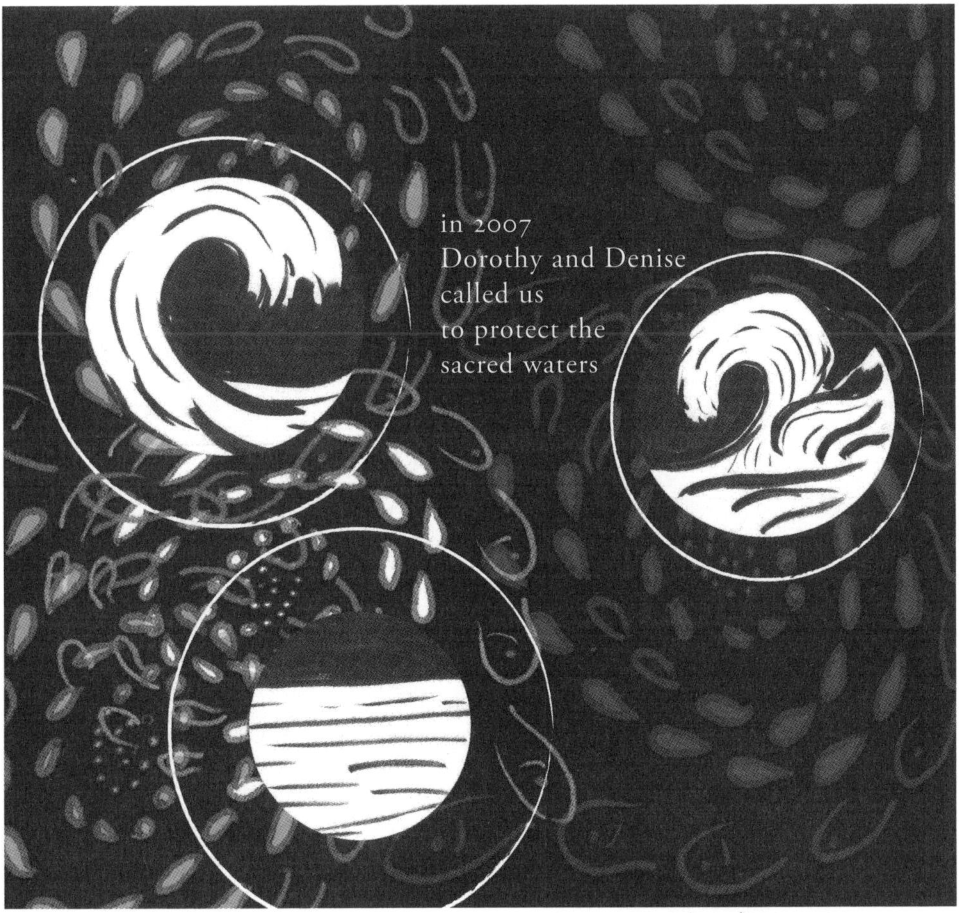
in 2007
Dorothy and Denise
called us
to protect the
sacred waters

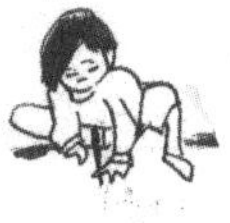

& here we are drawing, writing, talking
and walking our way to this

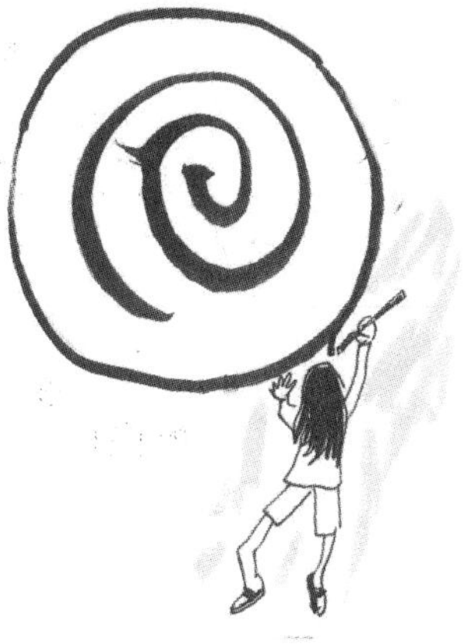

nourishing work of power shift,
paradigm shift

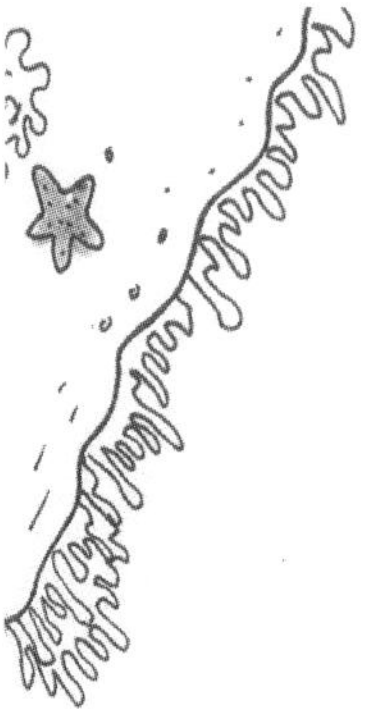

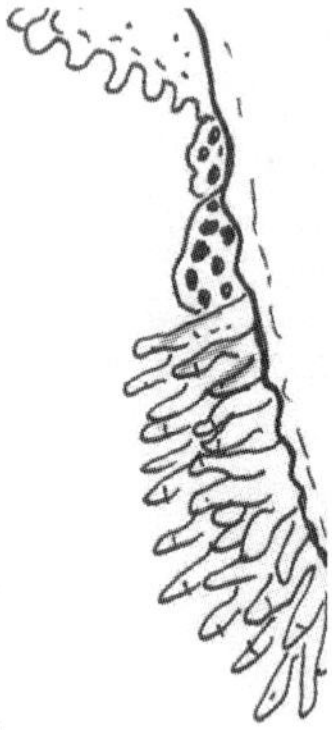

we live in a watershed moment

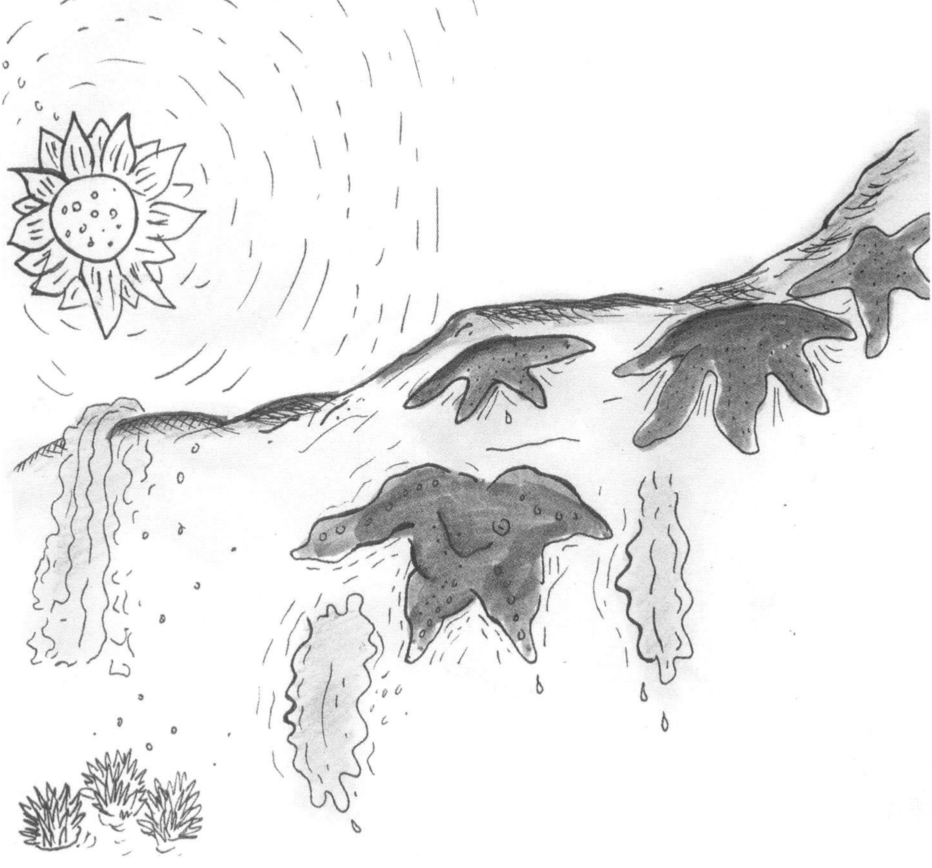

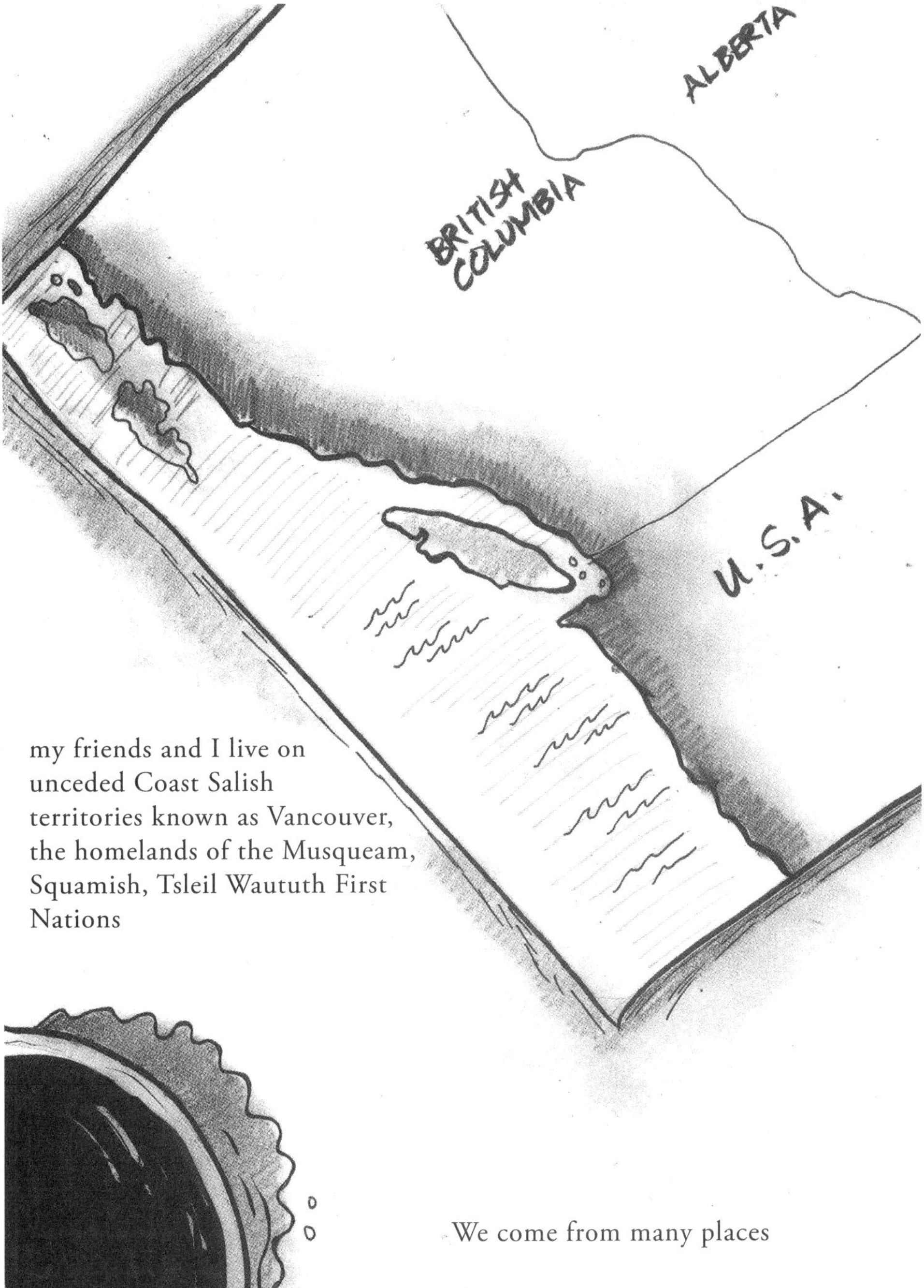
ALBERTA
BRITISH COLUMBIA
U.S.A.

my friends and I live on unceded Coast Salish territories known as Vancouver, the homelands of the Musqueam, Squamish, Tsleil Waututh First Nations

We come from many places

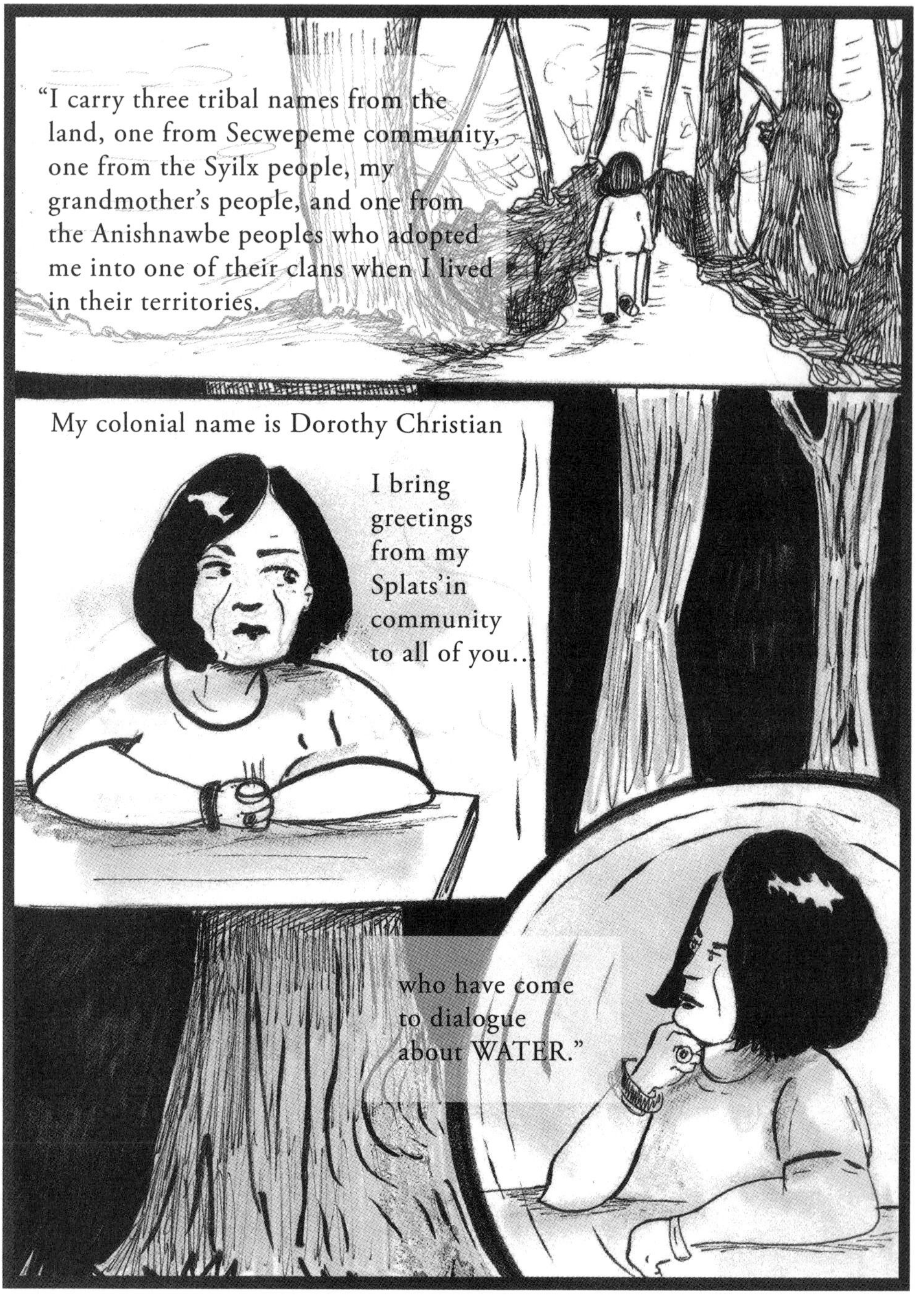
"I carry three tribal names from the land, one from Secwepeme community, one from the Syilx people, my grandmother's people, and one from the Anishnawbe peoples who adopted me into one of their clans when I lived in their territories.
My colonial name is Dorothy Christian
I bring greetings from my Splats'in community to all of you...
who have come to dialogue about WATER."

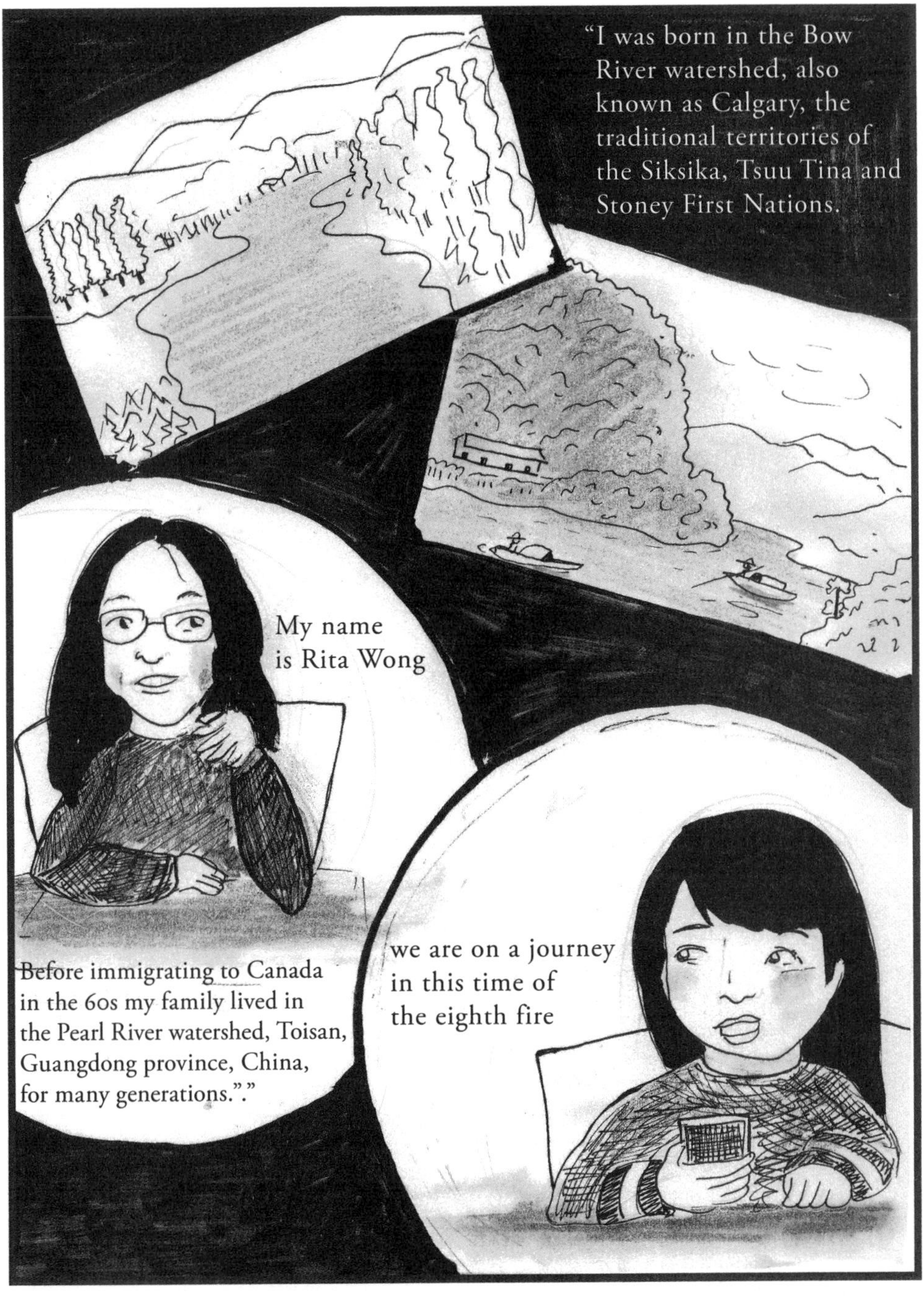
"I was born in the Bow River watershed, also known as Calgary, the traditional territories of the Siksika, Tsuu Tina and Stoney First Nations.
My name is Rita Wong
Before immigrating to Canada in the 60s my family lived in the Pearl River watershed, Toisan, Guangdong province, China, for many generations."."
we are on a journey in this time of the eighth fire

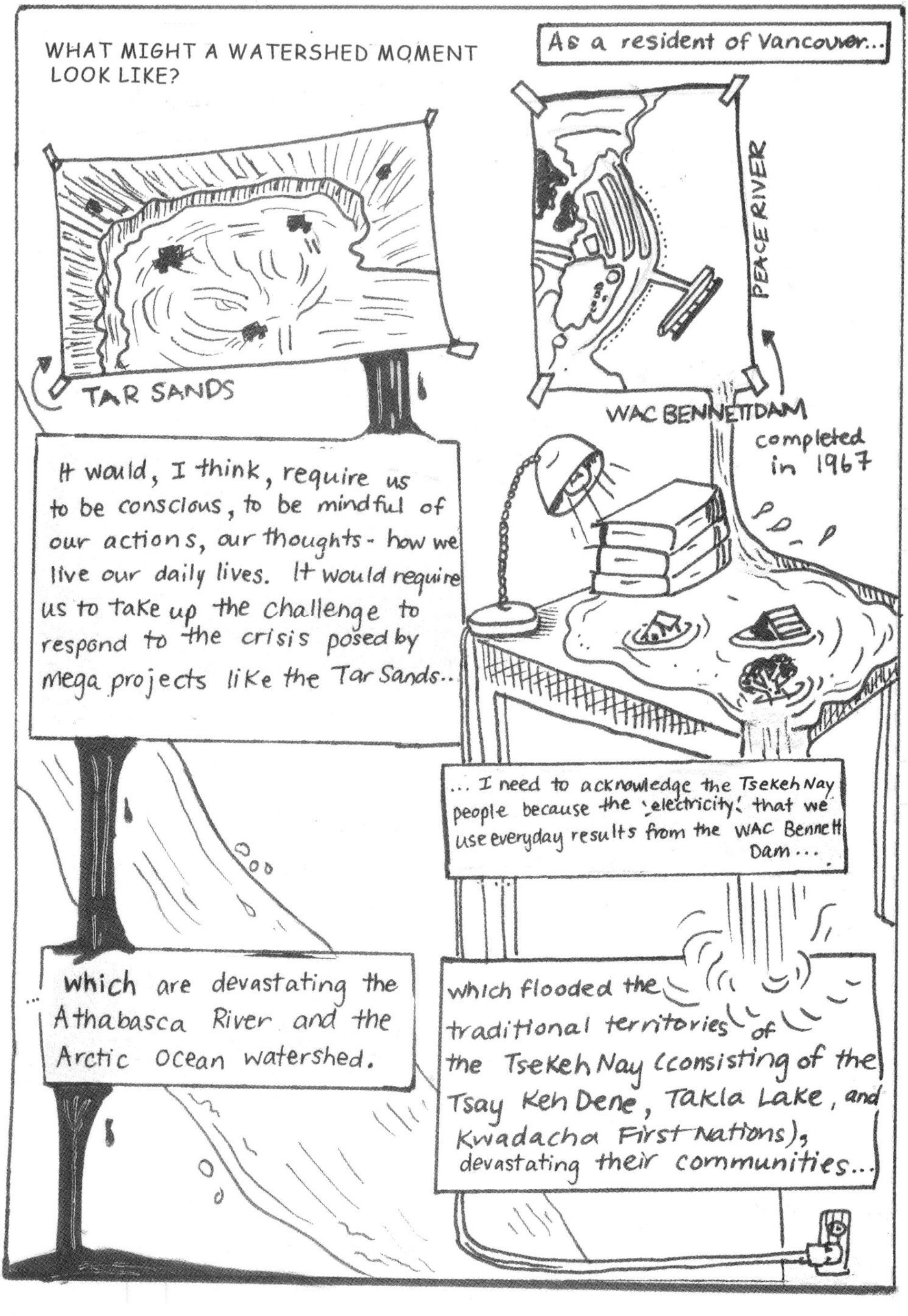
WHAT MIGHT A WATERSHED MOMENT LOOK LIKE?
TAR SANDS
It would, I think, require us to be conscious, to be mindful of our actions, our thoughts - how we live our daily lives. It would require us to take up the challenge to respond to the crisis posed by mega projects like the Tar Sands..
...which are devastating the Athabasca River and the Arctic Ocean watershed.
As a resident of Vancouver...
PEACE RIVER
WAC BENNETT DAM
completed in 1967
... I need to acknowledge the Tsekeh Nay people because the 'electricity' that we use everyday results from the WAC Bennett Dam...
which flooded the traditional territories of the Tsekeh Nay (consisting of the Tsay Keh Dene, Takla Lake, and Kwadacha First Nations), devastating their communities...

the proposed Site C dam would flood and devastate the Peace River's communities. BC can't afford this expensive mega-dam mistake. we need to plan for food security and encourage biodiversity in response to climate change. keep the Peace!

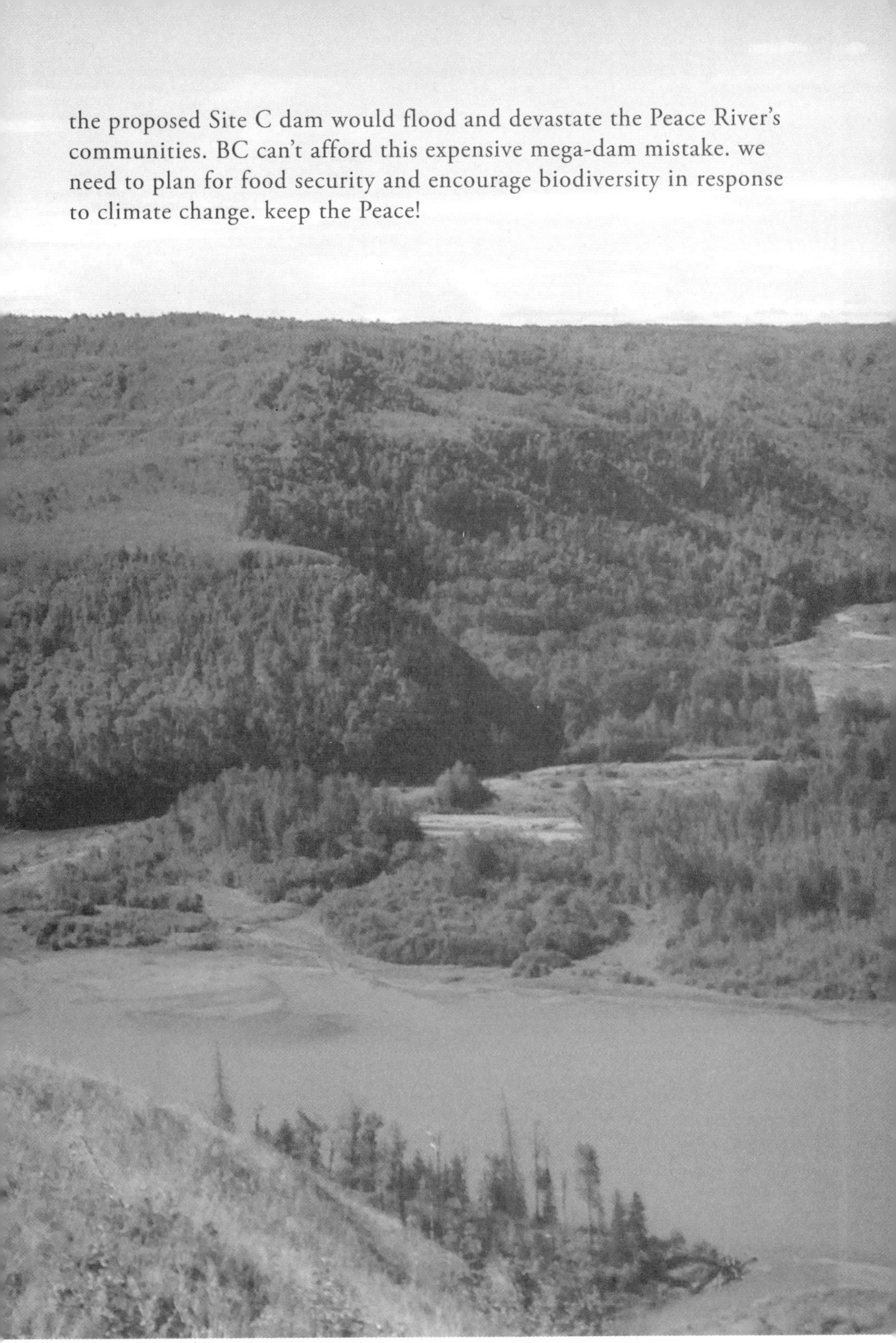

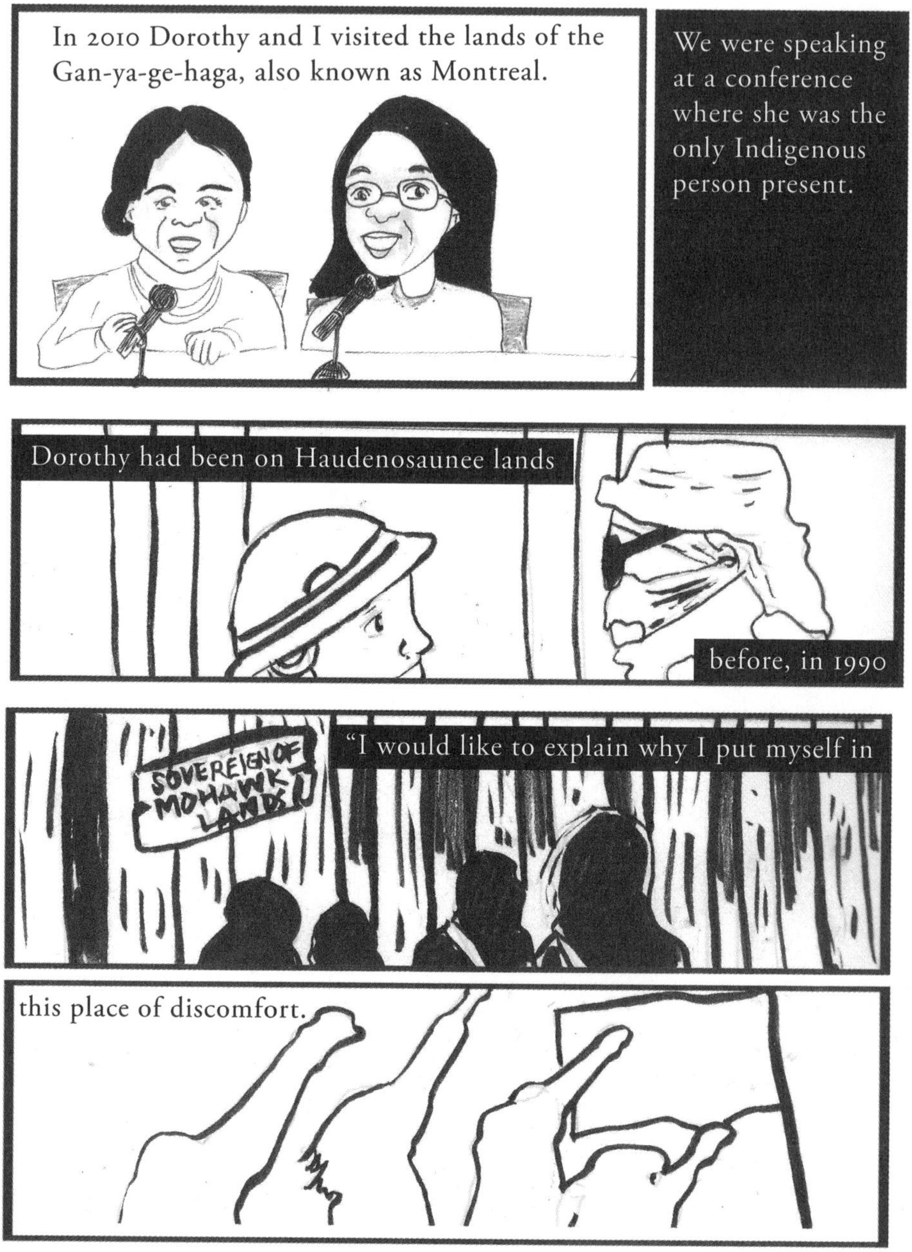
In 2010 Dorothy and I visited the lands of the Gan-ya-ge-haga, also known as Montreal.
We were speaking at a conference where she was the only Indigenous person present.
Dorothy had been on Haudenosaunee lands
before, in 1990
"I would like to explain why I put myself in
SOVEREIGN OF MOHAWK LANDS
this place of discomfort.

Over 20 years ago at the so-called Oka crisis, I worked behind the scenes with the Iroquois Confederacy negotiators (Mike Myers and Bob Antoine) in the communcations arena to raise international consciousness about the land rights of the people at Kanesatake.

Our current environmental reality is so urgent that we need to build alliances and relationships to work for the changes that are needed."

Dorothy has given talks over the years, where she asks:

"Who is going to be standing next to me when an army tank is coming at me?"

She also asked:
"Can you love the
land like i do?"

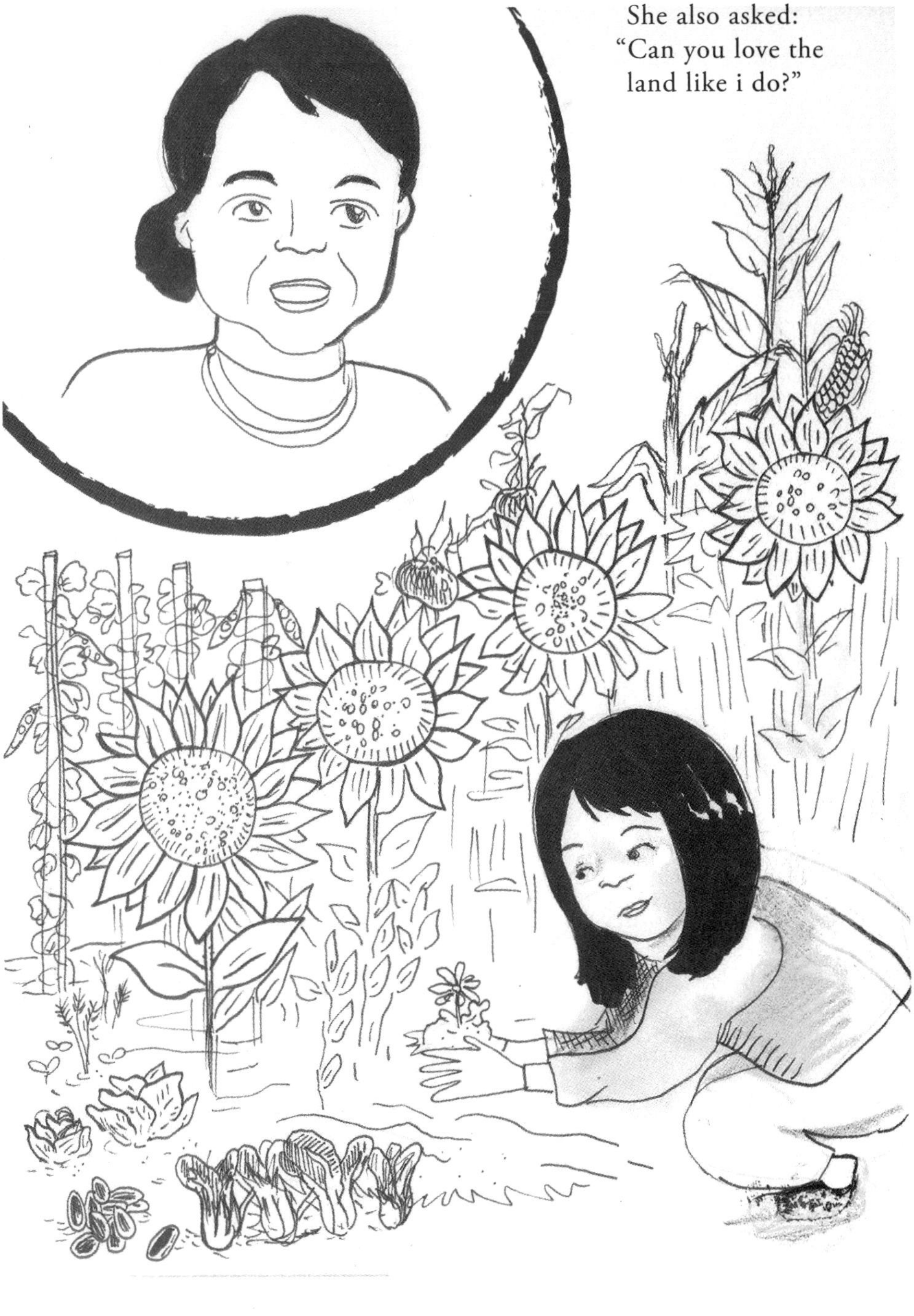

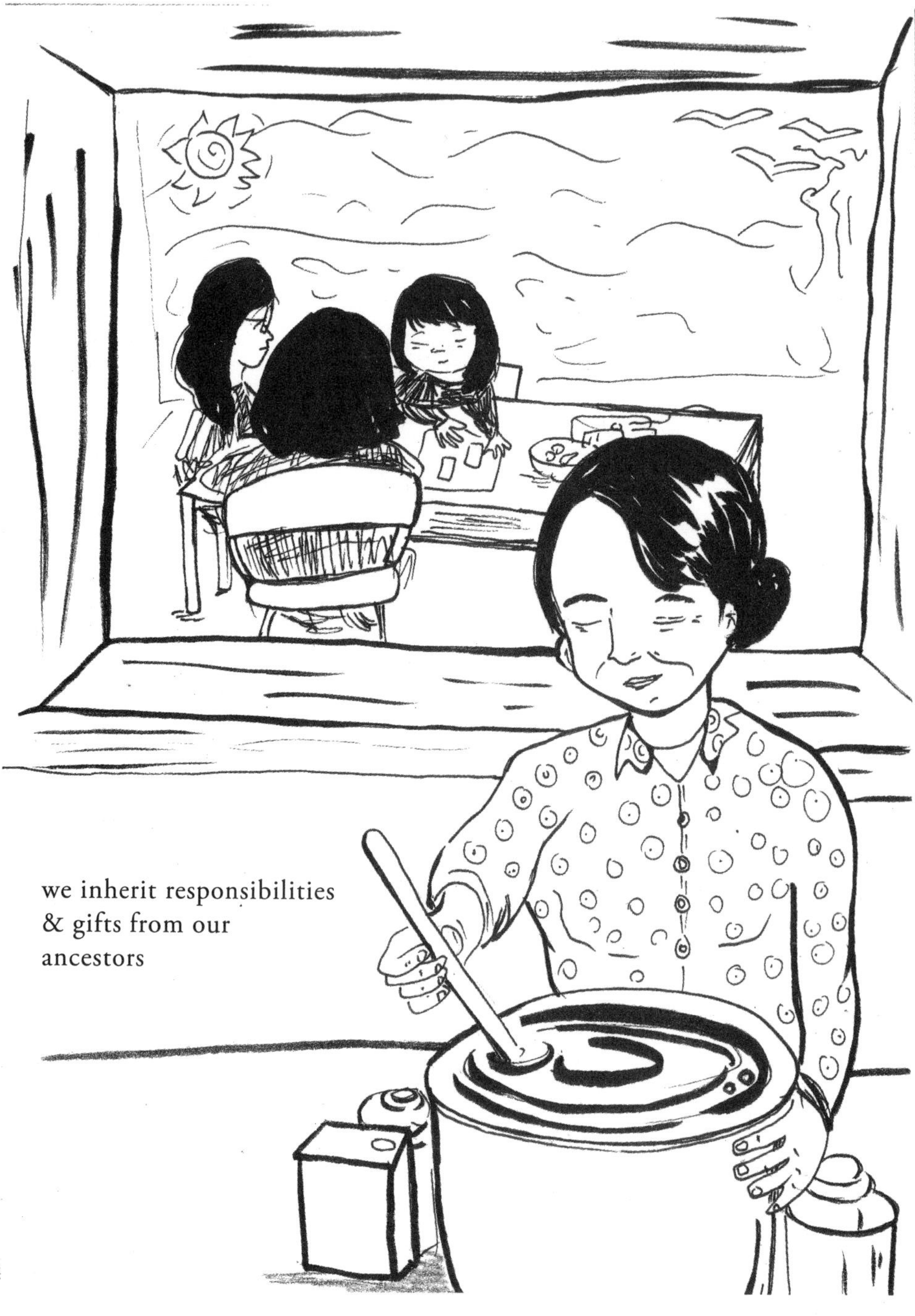
we inherit responsibilities
& gifts from our
ancestors

we bring these gifts to the cultural interface,
or the contact zone, of turtle island

how do we give back?

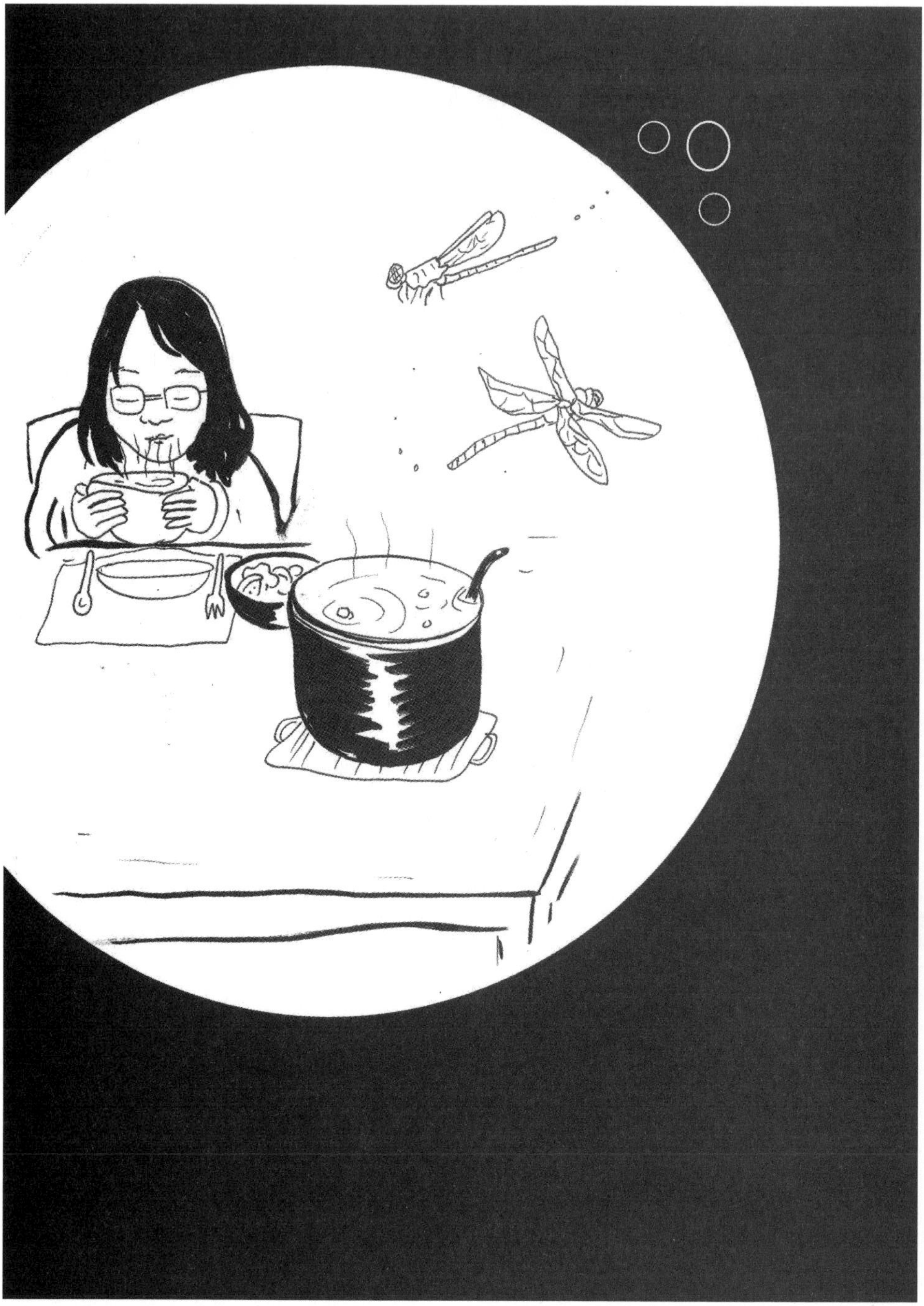

what do we pass to future generations?

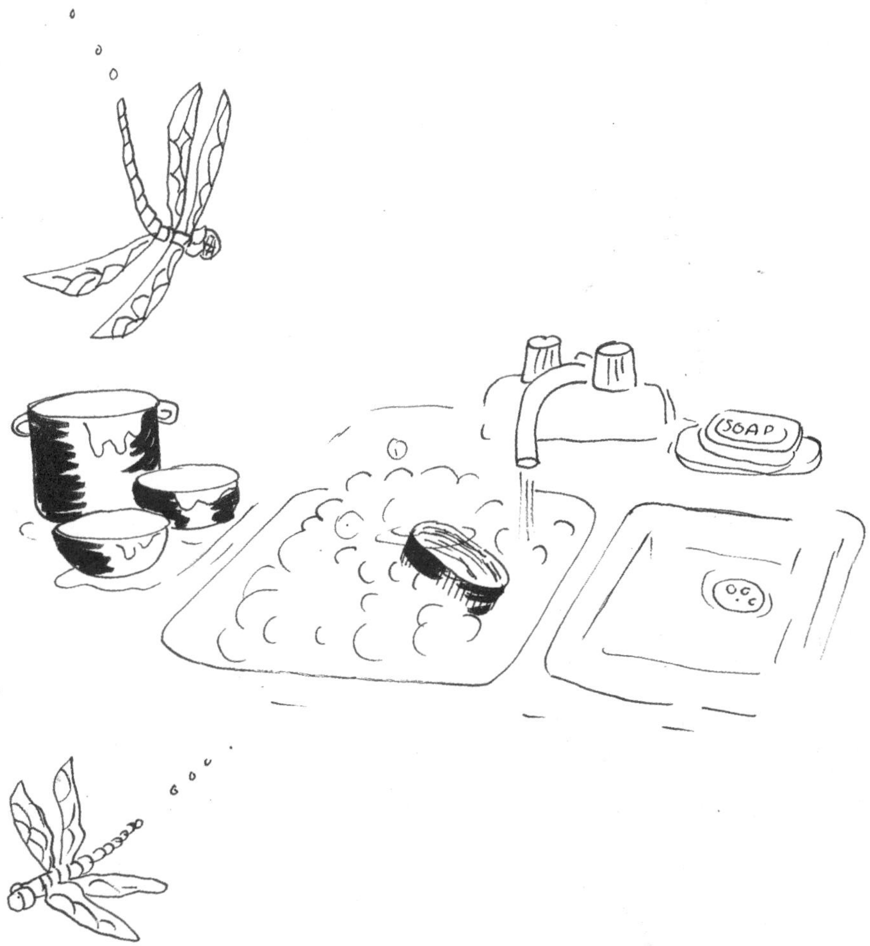
SOAP

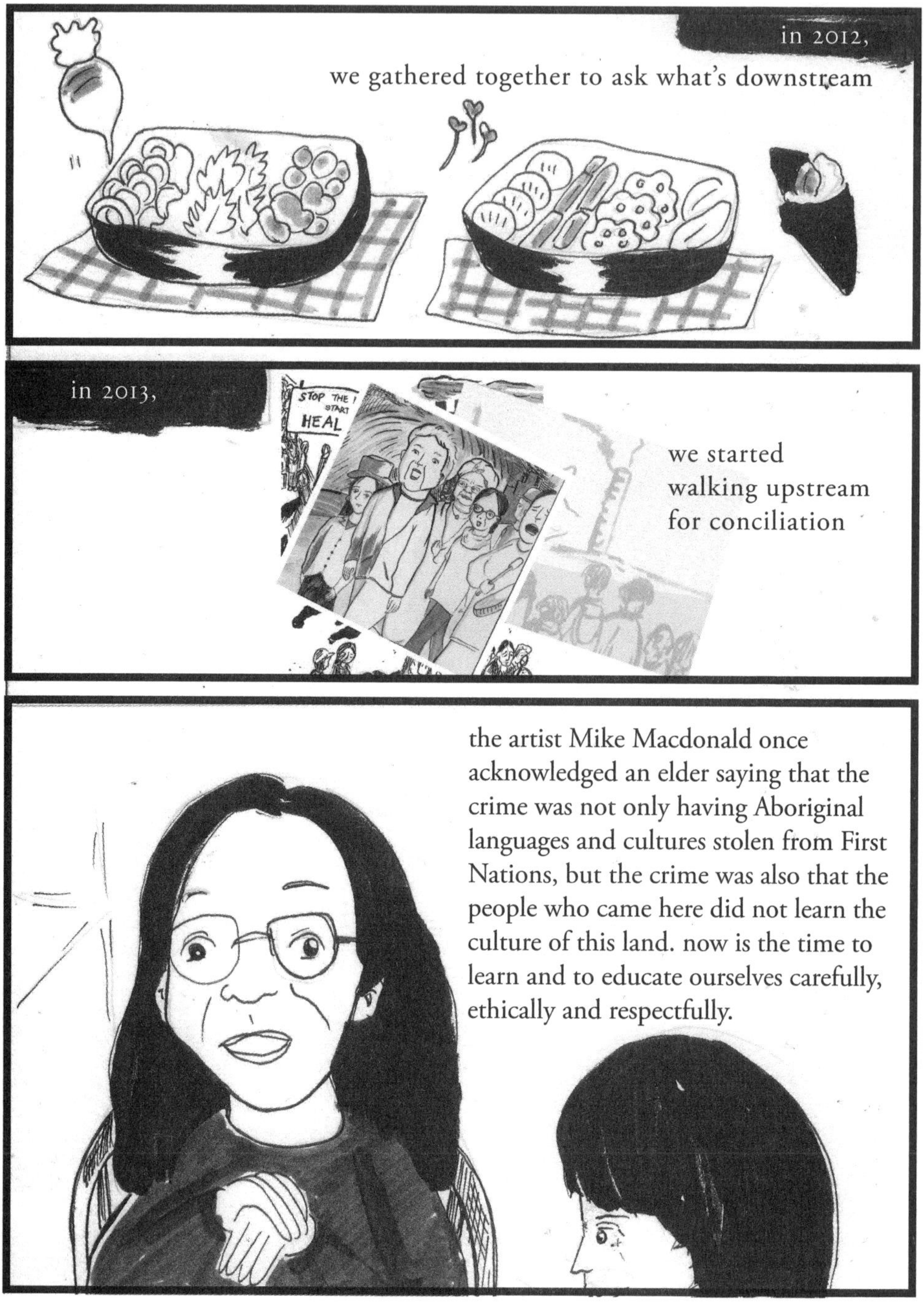
in 2012,
we gathered together to ask what's downstream
in 2013,
STOP THE
HEAL
we started walking upstream for conciliation
the artist Mike Macdonald once acknowledged an elder saying that the crime was not only having Aboriginal languages and cultures stolen from First Nations, but the crime was also that the people who came here did not learn the culture of this land. now is the time to learn and to educate ourselves carefully, ethically and respectfully.

how to decolonize and re-Indigenize?

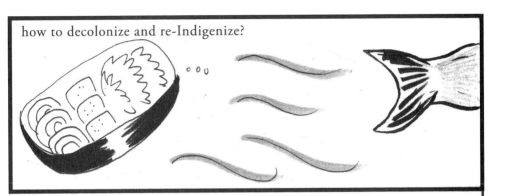

listen to the lands, the waters, the first peoples, whose everyday practices continue, despite colonial violence and the theft of Indigenous children from their families. today, some relationships are being rebuilt, renewed.

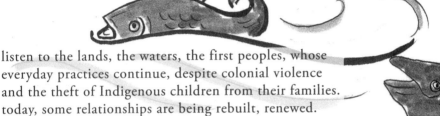

"I have to pick up salmon from my niece tomorrow"

An elder asked for some salmon because she doesn't trust the salmon up north after the disastrous spill from the Mount Polley mine

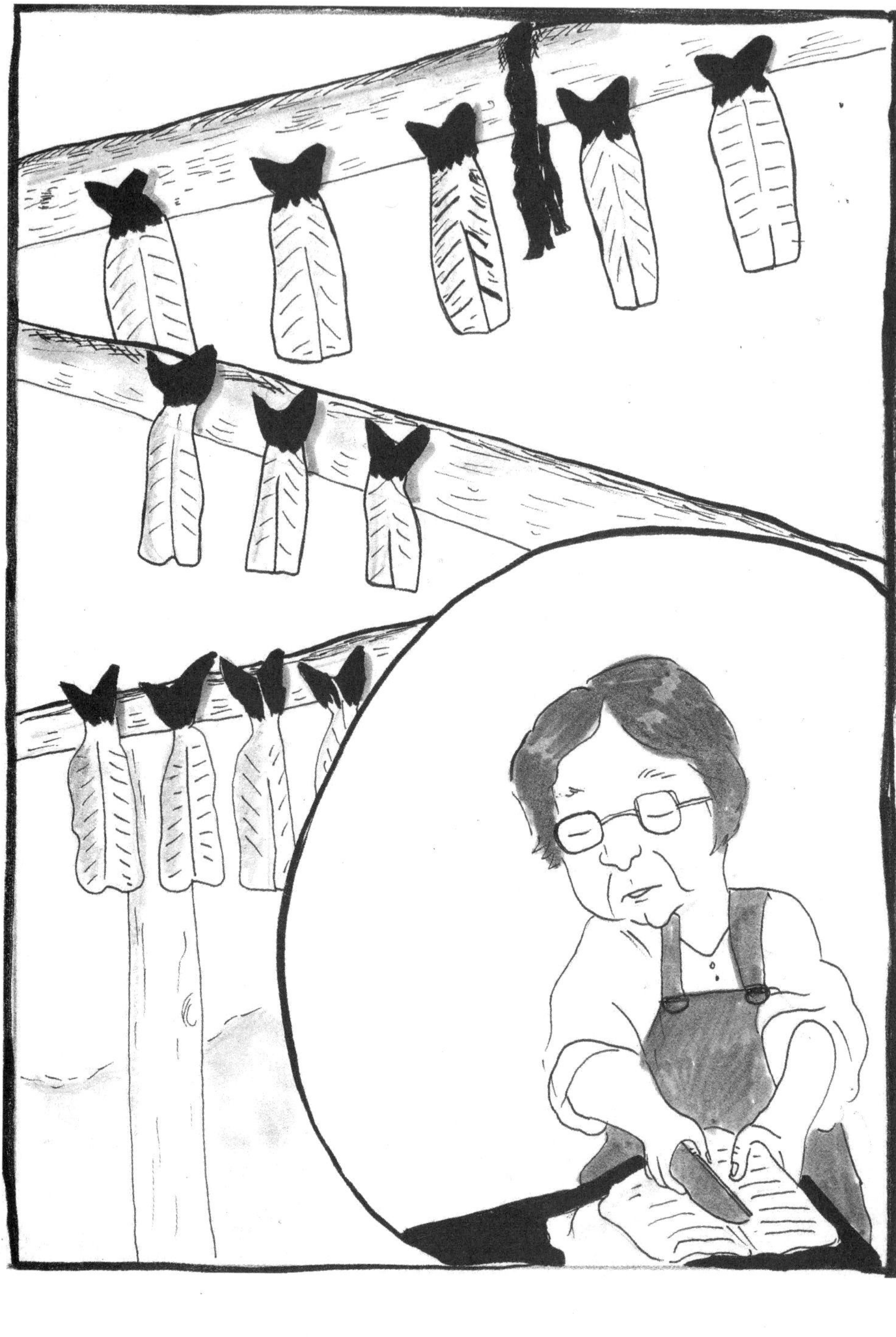

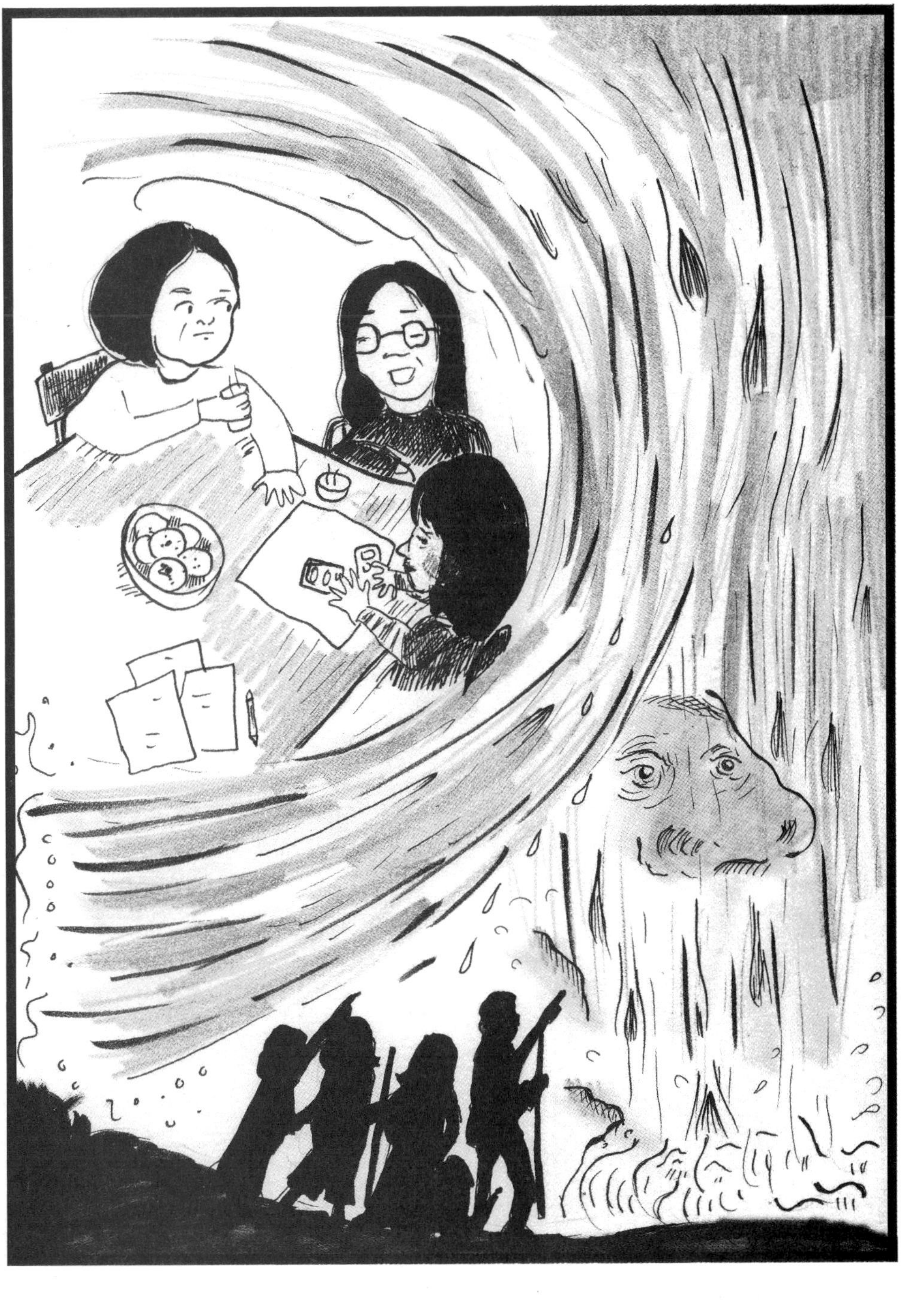

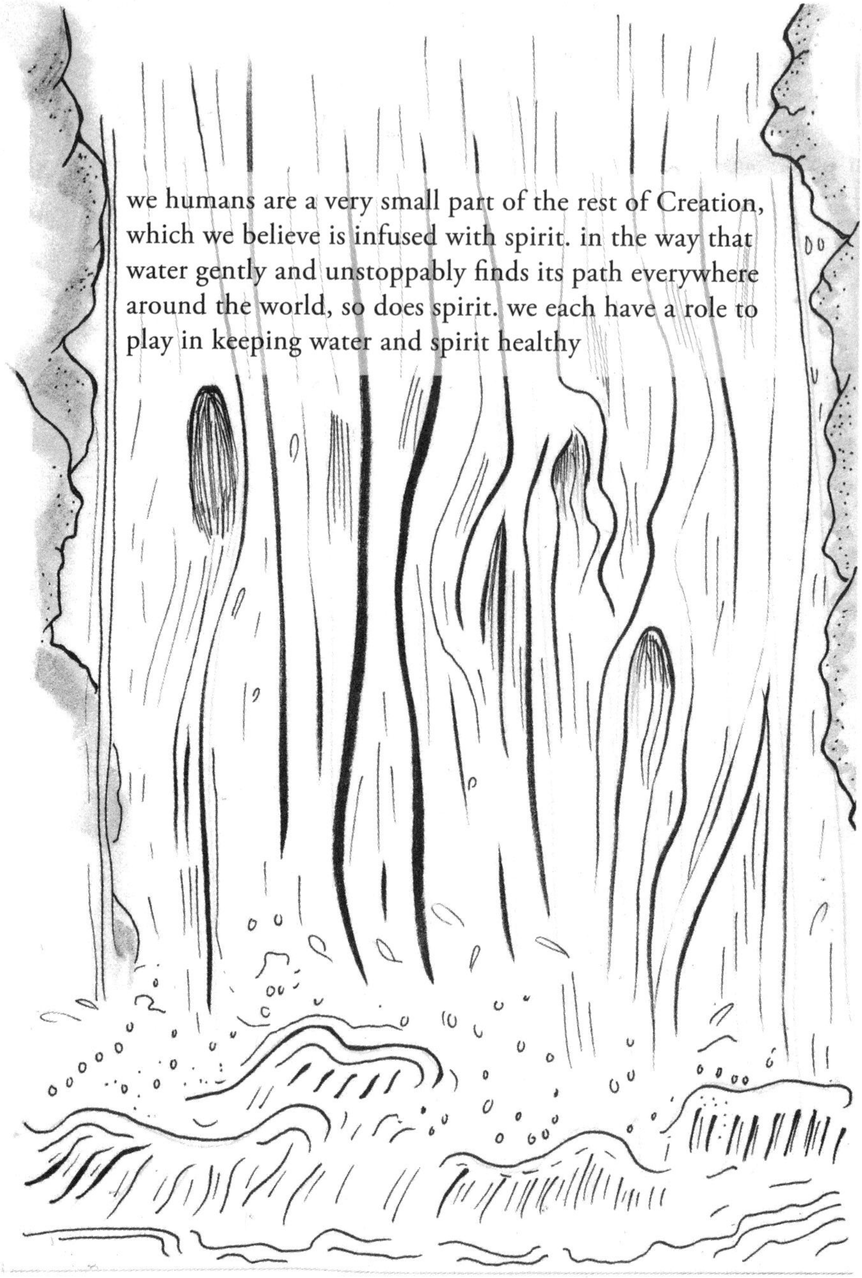
we humans are a very small part of the rest of Creation, which we believe is infused with spirit. in the way that water gently and unstoppably finds its path everywhere around the world, so does spirit. we each have a role to play in keeping water and spirit healthy

Aaron Wolf et al. "Peace in the Pipeline." BBC News. 13 Feb 2009. http://news.bbc.co.uk/2/hi/science/nature/7886646.stm.

Alanna Mitchell. *Sea Sick: The Global Ocean in Crisis*. Toronto: Emblem, 2010.

Alannah Young Earl.

Amazay: A Film About Water. 22 Nov 2011. https://www.youtube.com/watch?v=pypoI-54tLxg

Arundhati Roy. "Another world is not only possible, she is on her way." Truthout. 18 April 2014. http://www.truth-out.org/progressivepicks/item/23155-arundhati-roy-another-world-is-not-only-possible-she-is-on-her-way

Cardinal, Jesse. "The Tar Sands Healing Walk." A Line in the Tar Sands. Eds. Toban Black et al. Toronto: Between the Lines, 2014.

Charles Moore. *Plastic Ocean*. New York: Avery, 2011.

David Dodge, Pembina Institute, photo on page 42.

Dorothy Christian. "Remapping Activism." *West Coast Line 58* (Summer 2008): 15–19.

Dorothy Christian and Denise Nadeau. "Protect Our Sacred Waters." *Common Ground*. June 2007. http://commonground.ca/OLD/iss/0706191/cg191_waters.shtml

False Creek Watershed Society. http://www.falsecreekwatershed.org/

Ficus Chan.

George Poitras.

Kanahus Pelkey of the Secwpemc Nation. Freedom Babies. http://intercontinentalcry.org/freedom-babies

"Land Is Life: Indigenous Defenders Speak."

Featuring Ancestral Pride – Gwaiina and Xhopakelxhit sovereign Ahoushat / Snuneymuxw, Mel Bazil of the Wet'suwet'en and Gitxsan (whose words are in italics), Jackson Crick of the Tsilhqot'in nation, Freda Huson – spokesperson of the Unist'ot'en clan of the Wet'suwet'en, Arthur Manuel of the Secwpemc Nation, Kanahus Pelkey of the Secwpemc Nation, Khelsilem Rivers - Skwxwú7mesh-Kwakwaka'wakw, and Toghestiy of the Wet'suwet'en nation. 16 Dec. 2013. https://www.youtube.com/watch?v=iamLYN8CVBQ Organized by No One Is Illegal-Vancouver Unceded Coast Salish Territories, Streams of Justice, Council of Canadians and allies.

Lee Maracle. "Water." Forthcoming in the anthology *Downstream: Reimagining Water*.

Leila Darwish. "Update on the Mount Polley Mining Disaster – Imperial Metals and Government Focus on Covering Up Instead of Cleaning Up." Council of Canadians. 30 Aug 2014. http://canadians.org/blog/update-mount-polley-mine-disaster-imperial-metals-and-government-focus-covering-instead

Lost Streams of Vancouver. Vancouver Street Stories. n.d. http://vancouverstreetstories.com/lost-streams-of-vancouver/

Mike Macdonald. Artist statement. *Revisions*. Banff: Walter Phillips Gallery, 1992. 16.

Musqueam Ecosystem Conservation Society.

Nancy Scannie.

Pat Marcel and the Athabasca Chipewyan First Nation with the Firelight Group Research Cooperative. *Nih boghodi: We are the stewards of our land*. 26 April 2012. http://www.thefirelightgroup.com/thoushallnotpass/wp-content/uploads/2014/09/Firelight_Nih_Boghodi_Jan_2013.pdf

Peace Valley Environment Association. http://www.peacevalley.ca/

Rolling Earth Farm Retreat. http://www.rollingearth.ca/

"Sea star wasting disease likely caused by virus." CBC News. 17 Nov. 2014. http://www.cbc.ca/news/technology/sea-star-wasting-disease-likely-caused-by-virus-1.2838119

Shahira Sakiyama and family.

St. George Rainway. http://www.rainway.ca

Tar Sands Healing Walk organizers and participants. http://www.healingwalk.org/

Tardigrades: Adorable Extremophiles. SciShow. 11 Jan. 2012. https://www.youtube.com/watch?v=6HoE77TdYnY

Peter Warshall lecture on water. June 1995. https://archive.org/details/Warshall_lecture_on_water_June_1995_95P012

Stephen Hume. *A Walk with the Rainy Sisters.* Madeira Park, BC: Harbour, 2010.

Tsleil Waututh Sacred Trust. http://twnsacredtrust.ca/

Victor Guerin.

Violet Cheechum Clarke.

Xiaolan Zhao. *Reflections of the Moon on Water: Healing Women's Bodies and Mind Through Traditional Chinese Wisdom.* Toronto: Random House, 2006.

Excerpts from perpetual (the current title of this project) have previously appeared in the following places:

• *Alternatives Journal* 37:1 (2011): 15.

• *Front Magazine* 21.1 (2010): 14-19.

• in the *Asian Diaspora Zine* (unceded Coast Salish territories, 2015)

• and as a draft booklet at the *Healing Walk for the tar sands* (2013)

PHOTO CREDIT: Jane Slemon

Rita Wong is the author of four books of poetry: *monkeypuzzle* (Press Gang, 1998), *forage* (Nightwood, 2007), *sybil unrest* (Line Books, 2008, with Larissa Lai) and *undercurrent* (Nightwood, 2015). *forage* was the winner of the 2008 Dorothy Livesay Poetry Prize and Canada Reads Poetry 2011. Wong is an associate professor in the Critical and Cultural Studies department at the Emily Carr University of Art and Design on the unceded Coast Salish territories also known as Vancouver.

PHOTO CREDIT: Adam Blasberg

Cindy Mochizuki's illustrative work has appeared in *West Coast Line*, *Front* magazine and *Alternatives Journal*. Her short films and exhibitions, including AIR 475 (2014), have been screened both domestically and internationally. She currently lives in Vancouver, where she received her MFA in Interdisciplinary Studies from the School for Contemporary Arts at Simon Fraser University.

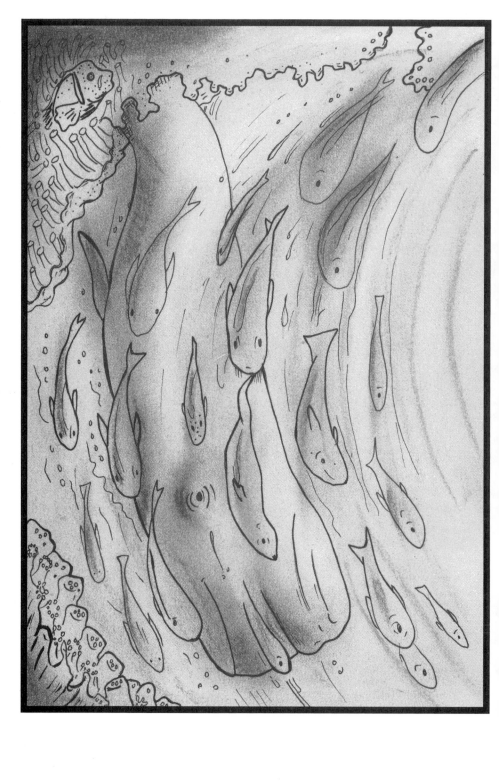